RESPONDING TO Acquisition Offers IN ESOP COMPANIES

THIRD EDITION

Neil Brozen
Tabitha M. Croscut
Nancy Dittmer
Alex Perry
Edward C. Renenger
Corey Rosen
Mark B. Russell
Randolph R. Smith, Jr.
James G. Steiker

The National Center for Employee Ownership (NCEO)
Visit us at **www.nceo.org** for more information about ESOPs

Responding to Acquisition Offers in ESOP Companies, 3rd ed.

Neil Brozen, Nancy Dittmer, Tabitha M. Croscut, Alex Perry, Edward C. Renenger, Corey Rosen, Mark B. Russell, Randolph R. Smith, Jr., and James G. Steiker

Book design by Scott Rodrick

The National Center for Employee Ownership
(510) 208-1300
www.nceo.org

First edition February 2011; second edition February 2016; third edition February 2023

ISBN: 978-1-954990-08-1

Contents

Introduction

Corey Rosen

ONE OF THE MOST DIFFICULT ISSUES for ESOP companies to deal with is the sale of the company. ESOP companies do get sold. A substantial majority of ESOP terminations each year result from sales of the company at a premium, although some companies are sold because they were in financial difficulties or could not manage their repurchase obligations.

ESOP companies routinely receive offers to sell to another buyer. Most often, these are not serious proposals, often coming from business brokers looking for potential acquisition targets or competitors seeking information. But other offers are more serious, and these must be considered by the board and, if the board determines they are legitimate and potentially attractive, the ESOP trustee.

The reasons why it is much more complicated to sell an ESOP company or respond to an offer to buy one are complex and numerous, but include:

- Many ESOP companies want to continue to be an ESOP-owned company, but fiduciary rules for the board and especially the trustee may force consideration and, in a few cases, acceptance of an unwarranted offer.
- Acquisition offers may result in the loss of jobs, company values, or employees having to work for an undesirable employer, among other unwanted outcomes. While the board may have some ability to consider these factors, the ESOP fiduciary has to look solely to

the long-term maximization of plan assets. There are no hard and fast guidelines for how to do that, however.

- If an ESOP company does receive an attractive offer, and the board and ESOP fiduciary do want to sell, they may need to seek other competing offers as well, even if they like the company making the first offer.
- Because of all the potential legal issues involved, when a serious offer is being considered, the ESOP and the board should have their own separate financial and legal advice. A fairness opinion is usually necessary, and if the ESOP does not have an independent trustee, most advisors would urge it to obtain one for this transaction. All of this will build considerable added costs and complexity into a sale, something that may well discourage all but the most determined buyers.
- Depending on how the sale is structured and the company's bylaws, ESOP participants may need to be able to vote on the offer.
- If an ESOP is sold, there are multiple issues to sort out. What if there are contingencies on the purchase? Should there then be an escrow account for plan assets? What will happen to plan assets—will they be cashed out or rolled into a successor plan? What if there is still an unpaid loan? How are suspense account shares dealt with? What if the buyer has its own ESOP? How are the plans merged together?

Most ESOP companies decide how to deal with these issues only when they come up. But a far better approach is to be prepared in advance with a thought-out plan. This will include a board document detailing the procedure for responding to an offer, one that may contain various features to help deter unwanted bids, such as stating that the company prefers to stay employee owned or independent. Potential acquirers would be sent a letter detailing requirements the company has before considering a bid and explaining the issues involved with the ESOP's role. This will help assure that all but the most serious bids are withdrawn.

If a company does want to sell, then it needs to go into the transaction understanding what ERISA requires, potential risks in not following strict guidelines, how the sale can be structured in various ways to maximize the value to participants, and what the company and plan fiduciary would like to see happen to ESOP assets.

About the Third Edition

For the third edition of this book, every chapter was revised, sometimes substantially, except the chapter 8 case study, which was replaced with a chapter on what you can do if your company doesn't want to be sold.

1

Fiduciary Issues and Practical Solutions for ESOP Company Boards When Responding to Acquisition Offers

Tabitha M. Croscut

WHEN THE BOARD OF DIRECTORS of an ESOP-owned[1] company responds to an acquisition offer, the members of the board should be aware of what their legal obligations are. Although ESOPs have been in existence for decades, many of the legal standards governing the conduct of members of boards of directors of ESOP-owned companies (in an acquisition setting or otherwise) hark back to a legal history that has little or nothing to do with ESOPs or employee ownership. This disconnect can cause a board to feel that the legal standards make little or no sense for their situation. This is not surprising, because these

1. In this chapter, a reference to "ESOP-owned" includes both a minority ESOP-owned company and a majority ESOP-owned company unless the text otherwise makes a distinction.

standards—which govern a board's duty of care, its duty of loyalty, the business judgment rule, and the basic legal framework underlying the governance of corporations in general—have historical roots dating to the Gilded Age of the late 19th century, although they have been revised over time through statutory changes and judicial interpretation. Understanding these rules is essential for the good governance of an ESOP-owned company, especially when responding to an acquisition offer, regardless of whether the ESOP is a minority or majority holder of company stock.

Basic Operative Principles for a Board of Directors: Sources of Law and a Brief Overview of State Statutes

The basic governing legal principles for board members arise from four sources: (1) state statutory law governing corporations; (2) a corporation's articles of incorporation (or "articles of association" or "certificate of incorporation," as they are called in some states); (3) the corporation's bylaws (or "code of regulations," as they are called in some states); and (4) the state's case law concerning board fiduciary matters such as the duty of care, the duty of loyalty, and the business judgment rule. The state law that will govern the internal operations of the corporation, including board matters, is the law of the state of incorporation of the corporation in question.

Because the board is elected by the shareholders (including the ESOP), it is logical to suppose that the board merely represents the interests of the shareholders and that the board will engage in the kind of constituent work that elected political representatives often engage in. But that is not always the case.

In closely held or private corporations,[2] board members are frequently shareholders and officers and view themselves more as partners to each other in the enterprise rather than as representing any shareholder's interest other than their own. The introduction of

2. This chapter refers to "privately held" and "closely held" corporations interchangeably. Both phrases are used to define the ownership of a corporation the shares of which are not publicly traded on any stock exchange.

the ESOP as a shareholder into a closely held corporation, however, creates a constituent where none had previously existed. Of necessity, the introduction of a new constituent should result in changed relationships between the board and shareholders. This does not always happen, though, and that presents a problem generally, and particularly in the context of an acquisition offer. For example, if an ESOP-owned company's board consists of directors who are also members of an aging management team, the board may be far more likely to view favorably offers to acquire the business than the ESOP would be. Such a board might view a sale as a quick solution to succession challenges versus focusing on the future value prospects of the company as an ESOP-owned entity.

Many state corporate law statutes include a statutory description of the general standards that govern boards of directors. The statutes generally require that a director will discharge their duties as a director in good faith, with the care an ordinarily prudent person in a like position would exercise under similar circumstances and in a manner the director reasonably believes to be in the best interests of the corporation.[3] What is of primary importance here is that the director is being held to the standard of an "ordinarily prudent person." The director is not held to the standard of an expert.

Because the director is only supposed to meet the prudent person test, the standard-of-conduct statutes also allow a director to rely on information, reports, and statements prepared or presented by one or more officers or employees of the corporation. To be able to rely on these reports, however, the director must reasonably believe that the person is reliable and competent in the matters presented. Directors may also rely on advice from legal counsel, public accountants, and other professionals, such as investment bankers. In addition, a board member is generally entitled to rely on a committee of the board of directors of which the director is not a member if the director reasonably believes that the committee is competent.

A director is not generally considered to be acting in good faith if they have actual knowledge concerning the matter in question that makes the reliance unwarranted. For example, if a director were a CPA and could tell that financial reports presented to the board were not

---

3. *See* Vt. Stat. Ann. tit. 11A, § 8.30(a) (2021).

accurate from an accounting perspective, that director would be held to a higher standard. Finally, a director is generally not liable for any action taken as a director or any failure to act if they performed these actions in conformance with the statutory section.

The Basic Legal Duties of a Board of Directors

In general, board members must fulfill three key duties: the duty of care, the duty of loyalty, and the duty to act in good faith as outlined under applicable state law. These duties play an important role in responding to acquisition offers. The following provides a brief overview of each duty.

The Duty of Care

The duty of care is codified in most state statutes; however, a handful of states rely solely on state common law. A relatively simple statement of the duty of care is that directors of a corporation have to exercise their duties in a way that avoids harm to the corporation. The duty of care requires that board members be attentive to the operations of the company. Courts tend to describe the duty of care as the duty to act as a reasonably prudent person would act under similar circumstances. However, certain statutory rules and the concept of the "business judgment rule" create some limitations on the application of the prudent person rule.

A director generally owes their duty of care to the corporation and its shareholders,[4] but this constituency may expand to creditors if the corporation is facing significant financial difficulties. In addition, some states have passed so-called "other constituency" statutes, which allow boards of directors to consider the impact of their decisions on constituencies beyond shareholders, such as employees, suppliers, customers, and local economies.[5]

---

4. *See generally* Dodge v. Ford Motor Co., 170 N.W. 668 (Mich. 1919).

5. *See* Conn. Gen. Stat. § 33-756(g) (2017); N.Y. Bus. Corp. Law § 717(b) (Consol. 2017).

The past decade has seen the addition to state statutes of the "benefit corporation" or "public benefit corporation," which is another type of corporate entity that expands the list of considerations and constituencies that directors can consider beyond the focus of shareholder value.[6] Benefit corporations have been increasing in popularity.[7] Benefit corporations are required to state in their articles of incorporation that they have a purpose of creating a general public benefit,[8] and that stated benefit can be set forth in the organizational documents of a new corporation or through a reorganized existing corporation. The definition of a "public benefit" differs depending on the state statute, but Delaware's statute defines it to mean "a positive effect (or reduction of negative effects) on 1 or more categories of persons, entities, communities or interests (other than stockholders in their capacities as stockholders) including, but not limited to, effects of an artistic, charitable, cultural, economic, educational, environmental, literary, medical, religious, scientific of technological nature."[9]

It is unsettled whether these statutes will protect a board in the instance it does not pursue a legitimate offer from an acquirer whose proposal is financially advantageous but would reduce employment, move the company, change the corporate mission, etc. However, such provisions might discourage some potential acquirers from making a serious bid. For companies interested in protecting their ESOP ownership, converting the company to a benefit corporation arguably offers the board greater latitude with respect to the constituencies the board considers in the face of an unsolicited offer from a third party. The more expansive list of public benefit considerations is likely to provide greater support for the decision by a board to reject the overtures of potential acquirors on factors other than purchase price (e.g., a loss of jobs or plant closure). While each state statute has its own nuances, it is currently expected that benefit corporations present another option

6. Not to be confused with "B Corporation," which is a private, third-party certification offered by B Lab.

7. Maryland became the first state to adopt and pass the benefit corporation legislation in 2010.

8. Vt. Stat. Ann. tit. 11A, § 21.08(a) (2011).

9. Del. Code Ann. tit. 8, § 362(b) (2022).

for companies that want a stronger defense against the pressures of selling to third parties solely to optimize financial return.

The Duty of Loyalty

If the duty of care is designed to ensure that directors do not act stupidly, then the duty of loyalty is designed to make sure that directors do not act greedily and do not put their own interests above those of the shareholders. Most commonly, we think of the duty of loyalty as coming into play if directors favor themselves at the expense of the corporation in entering into contracts with the corporation or if they take business opportunities that otherwise should have belonged to the corporation. The duty of loyalty is also directly implicated whenever directors are also executives if they are approving compensation matters for themselves, leasing or purchasing real estate from an executive (typically the former majority shareholder), or establishing special executive bonus programs like stock appreciation rights plans. The duty of loyalty could also be implicated if a director, especially one who is also an officer of the company, discourages an offer to buy the company on the grounds that it could cost them or other executives their jobs, status in the new company, or compensation. Alternatively, sometimes directors decide to offer to buy from the ESOP stock of the companies they serve, typically when the company is in financial distress. Would that be a decision for the best interest of the ESOP is it solely for the director's self-interest? The duty of loyalty is an immediate question in those instances and must be addressed and carefully considered to ensure a breach of such duty would not be successfully alleged by shareholder(s) of the company.

Fairness as a Defense

A board's defense to a breach of loyalty allegation is that the subject transaction was "fair." State corporate laws differ in their approach to considerations of whether the duty of loyalty has been breached, so a review of the applicable laws in your jurisdiction should be considered as necessary. When considering the defense of fairness, a court's review of fairness can involve a review of the result of the decision, the process, or both.[10] The total question of fairness involves fair dealing and fair price. In other words, when a court reviews a conflict-of-interest transaction, the court asks, "How would a stranger to the company have been treated in the negotiation (i.e., what would the process have been)?" and "What would the stranger have gotten for terms (i.e., what would the deal have been)?"

This sounds easy, but it is difficult for the courts to apply these rules because all transactions have fundamental differences. Additionally, courts will implicitly look at transactions in hindsight, so boards must be able at some level to anticipate the likely economic results of the transaction.

In general, if there are interested parties involved in the board's decision, the board will have to prove the fairness of the decision, such as the fairness of the decision to approve an acquisition offer. Approval by disinterested shareholders may shift the burden of proof to the complainant to show how such decision is improper.[11] Alternatively, if disinterested directors approve the acquisition offer, then the decision should be subject to the business judgment rule, discussed below, and fairness will not need to be established.

In the context of a board's decision to recommend or approve a proposed sale of the company to a third party, a common approach, especially for a board that has clear conflicts of interest (as discussed further below), is to obtain a fairness opinion from the board's financial advisor. This is an opinion separate from the fairness opinion that is provided to the ESOP trustee, so in this situation there are two fairness opinions at the closing of the sale transaction. The independent fairness opinion from the board's financial advisor allows the board to support its decision with the separate process and determination of a third party, versus just relying on the board's view of the sale transaction. If

---

10. *See generally* Weinberger v. UOP, Inc., 457 A.2d 701 (Del. 1983).

11. In Delaware, the courts have upheld stockholder ratification of equity incentive plans established for director compensation where directors are clearly self-interested, but only when stockholders approved the specific director awards and the plan was self-executing—meaning the directors had no discretion when making the awards. However, when directors exercised discretion and determined the amounts and terms of the awards following stockholder approval, the court denied stockholder ratification as a defense. *See generally In re* Investors Bancorp, Inc. Stockholder Litigation, 177 A.3d 1208 (Del. 2017).

obtained correctly, such an opinion can substantiate the fairness of the board's decision when the business judgment rule presumption might be unavailable, or it can sustain the board's burden of proof in order to apply the business judgment rule presumption, as described below.

Who Is Disinterested?

The law acknowledges that conflicts will arise, and in order to address a conflict under the duty of loyalty, state corporate law statutes generally provide that conflict-of-interest transactions can be approved if a majority of disinterested directors approves, if a majority of disinterested shareholders approves, or if the transaction is fair. Court cases, however, still seem to require that even if a transaction is approved by disinterested directors, it must also be fair.

One of the issues that can be surprisingly challenging is determining whether in fact a director is disinterested. For example, in one case the spouse, father, and brother of an admittedly interested director were considered disinterested, while in another the interested director's attorney was considered not disinterested.[12] Under the Model Business Corporation Act, a director cannot be considered disinterested if they have a family, financial, professional, or employment relationship with a person who is not disinterested if such relationship would reasonably be expected to impair the objectivity of the director's judgment on a relevant matter.[13]

Once the disinterested directors are determined, then the question becomes how many must vote on the transaction to ensure the vote is not voidable. Under Delaware law, a transaction can be approved by a majority of the disinterested directors, and a single disinterested director can approve a transaction,[14] while other state corporation laws require a majority of the disinterested directors plus a majority of quorum when there is a disinterested director. The Model Busi-

---

12. *Compare Rocket Mining Corp. v. Jill*, 25 Utah 2nd 434, 43 P.2d 897 (1971), *with Sarner v. Fox Hill Gate, Inc.*, 151 Conn. 437, 199 A.2d 6 (1964).

13. *See* Model Bus. Corp. Act § 1.43(a)(1)–(2),(4),(5),(b)(1) (Am. Bar Ass'n, updated through 2021).

14. Del. Code Ann. tit. 8, § 144 (2022).

ness Corporation Act does not allow a single disinterested director to act.

What about shareholder approval? Does shareholder approval repair everything? In general, the case law appears to say "no." Shareholders can vote according to their pocketbook issues. However, if the shareholders dominate the board of directors, then they may need to show that the transaction as a whole was fair.

If interested persons are both directors and shareholders, can they approve a conflict-of-interest transaction as shareholders that they could not otherwise approve as directors? The answer to this question also appears to be "no." Interested persons do not get some sort of special dispensation merely by changing hats. If they are interested persons as directors, they are interested persons as shareholders. If it would be otherwise impossible for the vote to be passed, then they should understand the courts will apply a fairness review in determining whether the transaction can be approved, and they should seek an outside opinion as to whether the transaction or decision they made is fair.

Effect of the Failure to Disclose and What Must Be Disclosed

What if a conflict of interest has not been disclosed? Under some state laws, if there is failure to disclose any significant aspect of the conflict of interest, approval by disinterested directors or disinterested shareholders will be void. Some state statutes, however, provide that even if there is a failure to disclose, if fairness can be shown, then the transaction can go forward.

What must be disclosed? The general rule is easy to state but not so easy to apply—the interested parties must disclose all material facts that other directors would reasonably want to know. Unfortunately, one is not likely to know what facts should be considered material until after the fact, so broader disclosure makes more sense, and directors should exercise all discretion in favor of disclosure.

The effect of a failure to disclose or the inability to have disinterested persons approve a transaction is that the courts will review the decision under the rubric of fairness. If a court is using this review standard, it will essentially substitute its judgment for that of the board. In contrast, if a decision were subject to the business judgment rule, then a court is less likely to substitute its judgment for the board's judgment.

The Business Judgment Rule

Many boards of directors have a vague knowledge of the business judgment rule and generally feel that just about any decision the board makes is made as an "expert" and therefore should be protected. It is understandable that boards have this view. However, the business judgment rule is not a hard and fast "rule" but rather a presumption that courts should not second-guess the business judgments of directors of a corporation who act on an informed basis, in good faith, and with the belief their decisions are in the corporation's best interests. The premise of the business judgment rule is that courts should not second-guess the business judgments of directors that have nevertheless resulted in poor results or with which reasonable minds might differ.[15]

While some states have adopted the business judgment rule by state statute, in most states it is found in case law decisions. All directors should review and consider the state law applicable to their actions.

The business judgment rule applies only to decisions the board makes; it does not, in other words, provide a defense for lack of attention. Moreover, the rule is not absolute. Rather, as described above, it creates a presumption. If a board decision lies within the realm of the business judgment rule (i.e., it is not tainted by self-interest), then it is up to the plaintiff to demonstrate that the board did not act in good faith or with due care.[16] If instead the plaintiff is able to rebut the presumption by providing evidence that the board violated the duty of care or the duty of loyalty (i.e., by showing conflicts existed), then the burden shifts to the directors to prove that the challenged transaction was entirely fair to the shareholder plaintiff. When the burden shifts to the directors, the court begins its analysis by reviewing the *process* by which the directors breached their fiduciary responsibility.

15. Franklin Gevurtz, *Corporation Law* (St. Paul, MN: West, 2000), 278–79. See also *Litwin v. Allen*, 25 N.Y.S.2d 667, 678 (Sup. Ct. 1940) ("[D]irectors are liable for negligence in the performance of their duties . . . [they] are not liable for errors of judgment or for mistakes while acting with reasonable skill and prudence.").

16. *See Aronson v. Lewis*, 473 A.2d 805 (Del. 1984).

In a seminal business judgment rule case in Delaware, *Smith v. Van Gorkom,*[17] Mr. Van Gorkom, as CEO of Trans Union Corporation, negotiated a deal to sell Trans Union for $55 a share in cash to a company controlled by Jay Pritzker in a merger. Under state law, the merger had to be approved by the directors and then voted upon and approved by the shareholders of Trans Union. The board of Trans Union Corporation was comprised of ten directors—five inside directors and five outside directors—and Mr. Van Gorkom was one of the inside directors. Four of the outside directors were corporate chief executive officers, and one was the former dean of the University of Chicago Business School; however, the court noted that none of them were investment bankers or trained financial analysts.[18]

The court ruled that the directors were liable for approving the sale transaction. In making this ruling, the court emphasized that the board approved the transaction after only a two-hour meeting during which Mr. Van Gorkom made a 20-minute oral presentation about the transaction. Copies of the merger agreement were provided to the directors with insufficient time before the meeting for review by the directors, and the board did not inquire into how the price was arrived at. The price, however, represented a premium over its previous $38 per share trading price.

Two justices in dissent argued that the *Van Gorkom* decision was essentially creating a form of strict liability for directors; notably, the board was composed of skilled business people, including CEOs of other large corporations and a former dean of the University of Chicago School of Business. The majority, however, determined that the process the board used was flawed. It was too cursory, notwithstanding the skills and experience of the board.

The important lesson of the *Van Gorkom* case is that the business judgment rule will protect a board when it has the right processes in place. If the board is composed of well-seasoned business minds but does not adopt a good process, then the board's decisions will not necessarily be protected by the business judgment rule.

---

17. 488 A.2d 858 (Del. 1985).

18. *Id.* at 868.

When does the formation of good processes begin? It begins long before a significant decision is made. It begins in the day-to-day activities of the board, with the board identifying the core aspects of the business that require the board's regular review and monitoring; it begins with the board establishing committees and other tools by which the board informs itself of key decision-making processes and determinations of the management team; and it begins with the board taking an inquisitive—but not inquisitorial—approach to the company. The board must be attentive; it should be a curious learner about what is going on with the company's business.

Dealing with Unsolicited Offers

Against the backdrop of the duties of boards of directors and the availability of the business judgment rule, we now consider how boards of ESOP-owned companies should approach the receipt of an offer for the sale of the company. In this context, it is important to understand the role that participants in the ESOP have the right to play in such a sale.

Participant "Pass-Through" Voting

Under Internal Revenue Code Section 409(e)(3), participants must be given the opportunity to direct the trustee of the ESOP to vote non-registered shares allocated to their accounts on all corporate matters involving "the voting of such shares with respect to the approval or disapproval of any corporate merger or consolidation, recapitalization, reclassification, liquidation, dissolution, sale of substantially all assets of a trade or business, or such similar transactions" as the secretary of the treasury may list in regulations. In addition to this legal proscription, some ESOP plan documents direct the ESOP trustee to vote unallocated shares in the same proportion in which ESOP participants direct the vote of allocated shares in their accounts.

Pass-through voting will require that the company and the buyer disclose a substantial amount of information regarding the sale transaction to ESOP participants to provide them with adequate information on which to direct the ESOP trustee's vote. This might be a problem for some buyers, while for others it might solely inform the structure of the transaction to use a stock purchase instead of an asset purchase or merger structure.

A few important caveats to participant-directed voting must be made at the outset. First, an ESOP trustee may be required to disregard the directions participants make regarding their allocated shares. The Department of Labor has written that the ESOP trustee should follow the participants' direction unless it can articulate well-founded reasons why the participant vote should be disregarded.[19] Further, in *Herman v. NationsBank Trust Co.*,[20] the court determined that the trustee could not blindly follow the participants' directions regarding the unallocated shares. Instead, the ESOP trustee had to make an independent fiduciary decision. Therefore, the board cannot rely on the participants of the ESOP to vote against a transaction, as the ESOP trustee might be required to override the participants' directive if, for example, the participants are only voting to retain their jobs versus voting to maximize their ESOP account value.

Boards should keep the pass-through voting requirement in mind when considering how to respond to unsolicited offers and drafting unsolicited offer policies to apply, which will be discussed next.

Unsolicited Offer Policy

Successful companies receive unsolicited offers to sell on a regular basis. Many of these offers are fishing expeditions designed simply for investment bankers or others to learn more about the company; some, though, are legitimate. In general, a board or a committee of the board has an obligation to consider bona fide offers to purchase the company. This is because the board's duty of care encompasses the need to derive the highest value for shareholders.

A board should consider developing a list of policies and procedures about how it will deal with unsolicited offers before offers are received, otherwise referred to as an unsolicited offer policy. In addition, if such

19. DOL/PWBA letter, September 28, 1995, cited in Brown and Kober, "Legal, Tax, ERISA and Securities Issues," ¶13.3[4][c], n. 108, in Robert W. Smiley, Jr., et al., eds., *Employee Stock Ownership Plans* (Washington, D.C.: Beyster Institute, 2007), vol. 1.

20. 126 F.3d 1354 (11th Cir. 1997).

policies provide for a committee of the board to assess bona fide offers, the board should be sure to appoint that committee. Perhaps the most critical detail of the policies will be identifying what kinds of offers will be considered bona fide. There can be no one-size-fits-all answer to that question. Following the standards and procedures set forth in the policy, the committee will need to determine what offers are bona fide in its best judgment. If the committee believes that an offer is bona fide and that further discussion with the potential buyer is necessary, the board should probably consider next whether engagement of an investment banker is necessary to ensure the board is maximizing the value to be received in a sale to a third party.

While maximizing share value would seem to require in all cases the engagement of an investment banker to run a full market process, there are some situations in which a market process could be detrimental. In some industries, identifying that the company is for sale might cause a reduction in value, or the timeline related to the market process might be too long and cause a reduction in value. Hence, while it is important for a board to consider the engagement of an investment banker, other considerations may be relevant when a board is faced with analyzing an unsolicited offer.

Other points that should be addressed in such policies include steps that should be taken to address conflicts of interest. First, if the company does not currently use an independent ESOP trustee, the board should consider engaging the services of an independent trustee as soon as possible so that it may protect the interests of the ESOP and its participants without conflict-of-interest concerns. In most situations, it is not reasonable for a company to ask an internal trustee to handle the fiduciary duties associated with a sale of the company, as the potential conflicts of interest for an internal trustee will likely be too great, and they generally lack the experience needed to fulfill the trustee's ERISA fiduciary duties with respect to the sale transaction. Second, the board committee appointed to engage the investment banker and the independent ESOP trustee and to negotiate any sale transaction along with management should also include outside directors to address conflicts of interest among board members.

While interested directors will engage in special board meetings and related conversations regarding any proposed sale transaction, the board will need to ensure that only disinterested directors are involved in approving actions related to the sale transaction in order to maintain the business judgment rule presumption with respect to those actions. Alternatively, for a board that cannot shift those decisions to disinterested directors, it will be important for that board to consider other options under applicable state law to "neutralize" such conflict. As discussed earlier in this chapter, that might require seeking shareholder approval and/or obtaining a separate fairness opinion for the board. The facts and circumstances of the conflicts and what is permitted under state law will be important in considering how a board with identifiable conflicts can successfully sustain its decision if challenged. Remember, if the board recommends a transaction to the shareholder(s) (or determines not to recommend a transaction) that a court later determines was an imprudent decision resulting from a breach of fiduciary duty, directors can be held liable. For that reason, it is important to address conflicts early on in the board's process.

In summary, boards should take steps before receiving an unsolicited offer to identify what will be considered bona fide and how the company will respond to such an offer, rather than waiting until an unsolicited offer is received to answer those questions. As part of that process, consideration should be given to additional steps that may need to be taken by the board to avoid potential challenges to the board's decisions due to conflicts of interest. Finally, in all cases, boards will need to be aware of their duties under state laws applicable to the decisions that are being made.

2

Responding to Unsolicited Offers to Purchase ESOP Companies: Issues for Plan Fiduciaries

Neil Brozen and Alex Perry

MOST ESOP COMPANIES routinely receive unsolicited offers to buy their company. The CEO is usually the person who receives a phone call, email, or letter from business brokers, private equity groups, competitors, and others. Many of the contacts from brokers who do not have a client and are simply trying to create business for themselves. They also may be bottom-fishing for their clients.

The initial response from most CEOs is to say that the company is not for sale or to not respond at all, and typically not inform the board of directors or the ESOP trustee. Is this the correct response? Is the CEO required to present the contact to the board for it to determine a response? Is the board required to inform the trustee of the inquiry? What if the broker represents a client who has a serious interest in the company and the financial ability to purchase the company? This chapter attempts to provide answers to these questions and address the ESOP trustee's role in the process of selling the company.

The primary duty of an ESOP fiduciary under ERISA is to act solely in the best interest of the plan's participants and beneficiaries and for the exclusive purpose of providing benefits to the participants and beneficiaries. Therefore, any offer received must be carefully evaluated by a fiduciary with the participants' best interest in mind.

The role of the ESOP trustee regarding the potential sale of the ESOP company will vary depending on the ownership position the ESOP has and the structure of the sale. When the ESOP is a minority shareholder, the trustee role is limited since the majority shareholder(s) can complete the sale without the ESOP trustee or the ESOP participants' support. However, even in this case the ESOP trustee will need to:

- conduct its own due diligence;
- review transaction documents and provide suggested changes; and
- prepare a voting information statement and coordinate pass-through voting to plan participants if substantially all assets of the company are sold and/or if the plan document requires pass-through voting.[1]

The Initial Response to an Acquisition Offer

Most CEOs believe that all unsolicited offers can be rejected out of hand since the company is not for sale. This response is not appropriate. The proper response is based on the validity of the offer. What constitutes a valid offer?

The most important considerations to assess the validity of the offer to determine whether it is a bona fide offer include:

- Is there a buyer, as opposed to a broker working without a client?
- Is the offer greater than the most recent appraised value?
- Does the buyer have the financial ability to purchase the company?

We strongly encourage the board of directors of an ESOP company to have a written policy that describes the process of what should happen if an unsolicited offer is received. This book contains a sample

1. This chapter assumes the ESOP is the controlling shareholder.

of this written process in appendix A. This policy can include a statement that a "sale of the company is generally not deemed to be in the best interests of the shareholders at this time," if in fact this is true. However, it sets forth a strategy for a response if the offer is deemed to be serious. This strategy includes identifying the prospective acquirer, price, terms, financial capacity to complete the transaction, and other relevant items. A serious acquirer should be willing to provide most of the information requested. In certain states, the policy may also discuss concerns about community, employment, or other value-based issues that the trustee would not be able to consider.

There are circumstances in which an offer that is less than the most recent appraised value should be considered. This may exist when the long-term prospects of a company have changed for various reasons, including technology changes in the industry it serves, lack of access to capital, inability to secure successor management, etc. For instance, if the primary product of the company becomes obsolete when a competitor introduces a better product at a lower price, the board of directors should consider a sale at a lower price than the most recently established fair market value. An acquiring company might value the assets of the ESOP company more highly if it can repurpose them within its own product and marketing capacity.

It is unlikely that a potential acquirer will provide a price in response to your request, as they normally do not have any data upon which to base their price and it is more likely that they will request financial information to allow them to provide a preliminary price. I recommend providing a very limited amount of financial data until you are satisfied that their other responses indicate that the potential acquirer is seriously interested and has the financial capability to complete the transaction. The limited financial data would include revenue, gross profit, and EBITDA for the current and prior several years. No information should be provided until the potential acquirer signs a confidentiality and nondisclosure agreement (NDA). *ESOP appraisals should never be shared with a potential acquirer.*

The potential acquirer should be expected to present the company with a nonbinding indication of interest (IOI) in response to receiving the high-level financial data. The following items should be included in the IOI:

- Price and payment terms
- Key indemnification provisions
- Escrow amount and length of time of escrow
- Target closing date
- Due diligence process and timing
- Remedy if the deal is not completed
- Absolute confidentiality

The board and trustee should receive a copy of the IOI. It is also important for the board to consider engaging an investment banker before signing the IOI to determine whether the board should seek other potential buyers. An independent committee of the board should be formed to deal with the sale if any board members have a conflict of interest, such as future employment or being lenders or warrant holders.

Buyers may not offer a specific price at this early stage, although they might suggest an EBITDA multiple based on a target EBITDA level. The board needs to consider the offer seriously if it believes that the IOI represents a bona fide offer (see the preceding chapter on boards and acquisitions in this book for more detail). In most cases, the board would then initiate a series of further discussions to get a better idea about what the acquirer might actually offer, and what the terms and contingencies of that offer would be. If these discussions are successful, the potential acquirer would then be asked to make a specific formal offer.

If the offer is, or likely is to be, financially well backed and is substantially greater than the current fair market value, the board should pass the offer on to the ESOP trustee. How much influence the trustee will have over the decision to sell will then depend on how much stock the ESOP owns and the terms of the ESOP. It is important to note that a premium, or even a significant premium, to the most recent ESOP valuation may be insufficient for the trustee to approve a sale. This is particularly relevant in early-stage or highly leveraged ESOP companies that often have significant stock price upside in the near term. This is discussed below.

Trustee Evaluation

The U.S. Department of Labor and Internal Revenue Service issued a joint statement in January 1990 that states the ESOP trustee is not obligated to sell the stock in an ESOP solely because the price is at a premium to fair market value, and can (and should) look at the long-term prospects of the company. Consider, for instance, a situation where the offer is at a premium to the most recent fair market value. However, although the company has had declining revenue and profits for the last two years, it expects its profitability and cash flow to increase significantly over the next five years as the economy improves. The trustee is not obligated to sell the stock if it believes the participants will be better off given the long-term prospects of the company versus the offer to sell at a premium price to the current fair market value. The board and trustee should consider the consequences if the opposite happens and the participants end up receiving much less than they would have gotten in a sale.

The trustee is required to make investment decisions based on facts and circumstances. It must weigh an offer against the underlying intrinsic value of the ESOP company and the likelihood of that value being realized by current management or a subsequent offer. It also must weigh the long-term value of the company against the value presented by the offer and the ability to reinvest the sale proceeds elsewhere. The trustee must analyze the long-term business plan of the ESOP company management.

In effect, the trustee must ask if the ESOP were sold at a certain price, usually a premium, and the money reinvested in a hypothetical diversified portfolio, how well would participants do compared to how well they would do if they stayed in the ESOP over the medium to long term, perhaps five to seven years. Moreover, the trustee can look at how the acquisition would affect participant retirement accounts in terms of what the ESOP company now contributes versus what is likely to happen in the new company. This is especially true with leveraged ESOPs, where shares often will be released to employee accounts at increasing values.

Say, for instance, that the company is contributing 10% of pay to the ESOP plus 2% to a 401(k). The acquirer has a 401(k) plan with a

50% match up to the first 6% the employee defers. ESOP participants would be far better off not selling unless the offer is well above fair market value. If the ESOP is leveraged, the effect may be magnified. The company may still be putting in 10% of pay, but shares are being released that, because they have increased in value, are worth not 10% when allocated, but 15% or 20% or more, a not-uncommon circumstance. A sale gives up all these potential future gains. On the other hand, depending on the circumstances, the premium may still benefit the existing participants because the premium on the unallocated shares can be allocated to participants either in proportion to current account balances or in proportion to pay.

The comparison is even more daunting for the acquirer if the company is a 100% ESOP-owned S corporation because the potential for future appreciation is dramatically enhanced by the non-taxability of earnings if the company is expected to be profitable. The trustee will engage its valuation firm to prepare an updated valuation, review the offer, and compare it to the future prospects of the company. This assumes they have the experience and expertise in dealing with these situations.

In some cases, the trustee may decide that the offer is simply too good to not pursue and will inform the board that it will support the sale. Most of the time, however, the process has just begun. The trustee may look at the existing offer and decide that certain aspects of it need improvement for the trustee to accept or even further consider it. The trustee might tell the board it would like the board to seek other potential bidders as well.

Companies with a newly formed 100% ESOP commonly experience high double-digit or even triple-digit stock price growth in the first few years as an ESOP-owned entity due to the significant leverage of a 100% transaction. This is somewhat unusual for a non-ESOP company that is not distressed. When considering expected deleveraging and potential tax savings (if an S corporation), the expected near-term return to ESOP participants could be much stronger than even a 100% premium to the ESOP value in certain situations. In this case, the board and trustee should evaluate expected performance under a "hold" scenario to understand what premium exists relative to an expected path of deleveraging.

For example, consider an S corporation 100% owned by a one-year-old ESOP with a most recent value of $1 per share that receives an offer of $3 per share. This would represent a 200% premium to the most recent value. However, it is entirely possible that extrapolating the forecast of the company would result in an expected value of $5 or $6 per share (or more) over the next 12 months. In this case, it could be appropriate for the board or trustee to reject this offer as insufficient despite the significant apparent premium on a percentage basis.

If the board decides to pursue or accept the offer, it needs to engage an attorney to negotiate the transaction. The acquirer will also need to be carefully informed about what must happen under ERISA to assets held in the ESOP. The entire process can take anywhere from a few months to a year or more. The board or a committee of the board will actively be involved in this process.

The trustee, not the participants, will make the decision to sell the company if the ESOP owns the majority of the company, the buyer is purchasing the stock of the company, and the plan document does not require pass-through voting for all sale transactions. The board must approve the sale and has formal responsibility to finalize the sale. If the ESOP has less than a controlling interest, then the board makes the decision based on instructions from all the shareholders.

If the ESOP trustee wants to sell but the board does not, or would only approve a sale under different terms, the process becomes complicated. Say, for instance, that the board's bylaws allow it to consider the employment or community impact of a sale. While the price looks good, it might still say no. The ESOP trustee cannot use these nonfinancial criteria. An example of this might be a situation where the board simply decides it does not want to sell, even for reasons its bylaws and state law do not allow, such as the preservation of management jobs. Or perhaps the trustee instructs the board to seek other offers and the board rejects this. The trustee then is legally obligated to challenge the board.

The ESOP trustee has all the rights of a shareholder since the ESOP is the legal owner of the shares of the company. However, the plan provisions could modify these rights. If the board fails to act in the best interests of shareholders, the trustee can take a number of actions, such as suing the board. In fact, the Department of Labor would likely argue that the trustee should sue to protect participant interests. Fortunately, there have only been a few cases that have been reported dealing with this issue. That may be, however, because internal trustees appointed by the board are not likely to challenge the board on this point, even when they arguably should. More likely is that boards have acted responsibly. Given that independent trustees have also very rarely challenged the board along these lines, the second explanation seems more compelling.

Because of the potential conflicts of interests for internal trustees, the NCEO recommends that companies with an internal trustee hire an independent experienced outside trustee to oversee the sale transaction. One result of all of the considerations described here is that hostile acquisitions of ESOPs almost never happen. Instead, ESOP companies are sold when the board and/or trustee decide it is a good time to sell.

Sale Structure

The structure of the sale normally determines the approval process for a sale of the company. Most buyers want to purchase assets and assume specific liabilities since this limits their risk against assuming all liabilities, especially those that are not on the balance sheet or otherwise identified. The sale of substantially all company assets requires participant voting on the transaction as it is one of seven transactions requiring "pass-through" voting to participants. Also, in almost all cases, as concerns the ESOP, there will be an additional tax on the transaction due to the sale of assets that would not exist if there were a stock sale. This requires that the price be sufficient to compensate for the additional tax.

The trustee is required to provide participants with sufficient information regarding the transaction to allow them to make an informed choice or intelligent decision when they vote shares allocated to their account. This information statement can be prepared by the trustee and its legal advisor and reviewed by the company and its legal advisor or vice versa. The trustee has the authority to determine the final document that is distributed to participants along with their voting instructions and directions.

The information statement needs to be written so participants can understand it. Most information statements will include a factual explanation of the transaction; analysis of the transaction; recommendations by management, the board, and the trustee; current financial statements and a fairness opinion; and participants' rights to direct the trustee. Many trustees will meet with groups of participants to review and discuss the information statement and, more importantly, respond to their questions.

The trustee must ensure that the information provided in the information statement or during participant meetings is not false or misleading. The trustee must also monitor the solicitation of votes to ensure participants are not subject to improper pressure or influence from management and to maintain confidentiality of the voting instructions from the participants by having the voting instructions sent directly to the trustee. Votes should be tallied off-site, and management and the board should not have access in any way to individual ballots. Having an outside accounting or administrative firm or independent trustee do the counting is highly desirable.

A participant vote provides direction to the trustee. The trustee is not legally obligated to follow the vote and should not do so if it believes the participant instructions clearly are not in the best interests of the plan participants. Future employment is likely to be a factor to active participants and specifically is not allowed to be considered by the trustee in its voting. The Department of Labor has indicated, however, that participant directions should receive great deference and should be overturned only if the fiduciary finds they are clearly in violation of ERISA requirements.[2]

Another issue that may arise in pass-through voting relates to the voting of shares on which no instructions are received, invalid voting instructions, and voting for unallocated shares. The plan document typically provides direction in these situations and can authorize the board to direct the trustee, authorize the trustee to follow the valid directions, or provide another option. The board can amend the plan to address this issue.

---

2. Department of Labor letter to Citizens & Southern Trust Company (February 23, 1989); DOL Information Letter re: Pass-through Voting Provisions in Collectively Bargained Employee Stock Ownership Plans, to Ian D. Lanoff on behalf of AFL-CIO (September 29, 1995).

Economically, the ESOP can sometimes be less concerned than a buyer with respect to asset vs. stock sale structure since it is not a taxpayer; however, asset sales of ESOP companies can add complexity time, and advisor cost to the sale process. As a result, many ESOP sellers prefer to sell the company stock as opposed to selling company assets. This structure is easier than an asset sale and does not require pass-through voting to participants because the trustee votes on the sale. Some ESOP plan documents and boards of directors provide for pass-through voting even when it is not required by ERISA.

Final Resolution

The key terms that were negotiated in the letter of intent (LOI) can be considered as the end of the first phase of the negotiation process, not the end of negotiations. The LOI will allow the attorney responsible for drafting the transaction documents to have sufficient information to create an initial draft. The fun really starts when the trustee and its legal advisor revise the draft purchase agreement and other related documents.

The most significant terms of the purchase agreement are:

- *Purchase price.*
- *Purchase price adjustments, which can include clawbacks, escrow, and earnouts.* These variable purchase price components can be subject to significant trustee input to ensure the ESOP receives appropriate proceeds such that participants are not dependent on future ownership to realize. ESOPs as sellers can be less willing to accept significant variable structures than an equivalent non-ESOP owner.
- *Representations and warranties.* The ESOP will rely on the representations and warranties provided by the company.
- *Indemnification.*
- *Limitations on liability.* The amount of time the buyers have to make a claim, the minimum amount of the claim (baskets), and the maximum amount of the claims (caps).
- *Conditions (precedent and subsequent).* They may include a fairness opinion and financing adequacy or terms.

- *Covenants (negative and otherwise).*
- *Treatment of the ESOP.* Will the plan be terminated and its assets distributed to participants (and, if so, when and under what escrow conditions)? How will forfeitures occurring before the termination but not distributed until after the termination of the ESOP be allocated? Will the ESOP be converted to a profit-sharing, 401(k), or other retirement plan in the new company, or merged into the buyer's ESOP? (See the chapter by Nancy Dittmer in this book on what can happen to the assets of an ESOP after a sale.)
- *Treatment of assets remaining after repaying the ESOP loan.* If the ESOP acquisition loan is not paid off before the sale and the purchase price is such that there will be assets left after paying off the debt, will those be allocated to participants as "income" or treated as an allocation of a contribution? What is the date of determining who is a participant?

Responding to an Offer: Step by Step

Many ESOP CEOs receive unsolicited offers to buy their company via phone calls or letters. While most of these contacts are a waste of time, they could be a real opportunity, and failure to respond appropriately to legitimate offers could cause unwanted exposure to charges of failure to meet obligations as a plan fiduciary. What follows largely reiterates what has already been discussed but puts it in a step-by-step process all trustees should follow.

The board should have a written policy for responding to unsolicited offers that sets forth a process for management and the board to follow. The initial objective is to separate the serious prospective buyers from those that are just "kicking the tires" or "bottom fishing." Requiring the interested party to provide significant information is one method to evaluate whether they are serious.

The board must take all bona fide offers seriously. It needs to analyze the offer, perhaps with the assistance of a financial advisor/valuation firm. The business judgment rule requires the board to act on an informed basis, in good faith, and in the best interests of the corporate shareholders. The board also needs to follow the "entire fairness" doctrine and "fair price" considerations. The board may want to form an independent committee to evaluate the offer as well as engage its own legal advisor and inform the trustee once it determines there is a bona fide offer.

The board or the CEO should request a nonbinding indication of intent (IOI) from a prospective acquirer. No information, especially high-level financial data, should be provided until the prospect signs a confidentiality and nondisclosure agreement. The IOI should include price and payment terms; indemnification provisions; the escrow amount and length of time; the target closing date; the due diligence process and timing; a remedy if the deal is not completed; and absolute confidentiality. The board should negotiate the best terms possible in the IOI and not sign it if the board cannot obtain the terms it wants.

The trustee will encourage the board to engage an investment banker to evaluate the offer and develop a strategy to solicit other potential buyers. The trustee will engage its own valuation advisor, usually the firm that has prepared the appraisal reports, and its own legal advisor. It is critical for the trustee, board, and management and their advisors to communicate with each other.

The trustee is not required to sell the company simply if a premium price is being offered. It is required to manage plan assets prudently and for the sole interests of plan participants and beneficiaries. The trustee needs to recognize that the ESOP is designed to provide retirement income and may consider the long-term prospects of the ESOP company.

The structure of the sale determines the approval process required. The sale of substantially all company assets will require pass-through participant voting when the trustee votes on the sale of company stock. The plan document may require, or the board may provide for, pass-through voting on a sale of stock.

The trustee is responsible for the information statement (or proxy) that it will distribute to all participants. This document can be prepared by the company's attorney or the trustee's attorney. The trustee is required to make sure participants have sufficient information to make an informed, intelligent decision and that they have sufficient time to decide. The company and trustee may also want to make presentations to participants so they can directly pose questions to the trustee.

Participants provide voting directions to the trustee when they submit their vote. The trustee can ignore the voting direction and vote in favor of what the trustee believes is in the best interests of the participants. This situation could occur if participants vote against a sale solely because they believe their future employment is at risk. The trustee cannot consider future employment in voting for or against the transaction and should not follow the voting instructions against a sale if it believes the sale is in the best interest of plan participants.

The attorney drafting the purchase agreement will use the terms in the letter of intent as the basis for drafting the initial draft. The purchase agreement contains the final terms of the transaction, including the purchase price, purchase price adjustments, representations and warranties, indemnification provisions, limitations on liability, conditions precedent and subsequent, covenants, and treatment of the ESOP.

3

Evaluating Offers to ESOP Companies: The Case for Engaging an Investment Banker

Mark B. Russell

NEIL BROZEN'S CHAPTER IN THIS BOOK on responding to unsolicited offers to purchase ESOP companies notes that:

- The board of directors needs "to analyze the offer, perhaps with the assistance of a financial advisor/valuation firm."
- "The trustee will encourage the board to engage an investment banker to evaluate the offer and develop a strategy to solicit other potential buyers."
- "The trustee might tell the board it would like the board to seek other potential bidders as well."

This advice is sound. Whether a company is ESOP-owned, family owned, or owned by a private equity fund, shareholders do better in a professionally managed competitive sales process than when negotiating with a single buyer. Shareholders receive significantly more consideration after running a sales process compared to the price that was offered before the competitive process was conducted. There is material support for this assertion. First and foremost is the fact that private equity firms that are regularly in the business of buying and selling portfolio companies almost always use investment bankers to help sell their portfolio companies. One recent survey of private equity firms active in the middle market found that private equity firms use an investment banker 94% of the time when selling their own middle-market portfolio companies.[1] As further support, consider that this same study also found that private equity firms estimate that they end up paying 1x EBITDA (earnings before interest, taxes, depreciation and amortization) more on average when an investment banker is used by the seller (with answers ranging from 0.5x to 2x EBITDA, but never the same or less). Finally, a 2016 study by a professor at Fairfield University surveying 85 business owners who used investment bankers to sell their privately held companies between 2011 and 2016 found that all respondents said their investment banker added value to the business sale process, and 84% of respondents stated the final sale price was equal to or higher than the initial sale price estimate provided by the investment banker.[2]

Hiring an investment banker does more than increase total consideration. It is also has a positive impact on other, more difficult to measure benefits that are very important, such as:

- introducing a wider universe of potential buyers/investors, including both strategic as well as financial buyers, to identify the "right fit" from a business model and a cultural perspective;
- improving key terms of the transaction beyond just consideration;
- helping to maximize transaction certainty;
- establishing a formal environment of confidentiality;

1. HighBank Advisors, "Selling Your Business: Separating Myth from Reality and the Importance of Hiring an Experienced Investment Banker," *SmartCEO*, http://smartceo.com/highbank-selling-your-business-separating-myth-from-reality-and-the-importance-of-hiring-an-experienced-investment-banker/.
2. Michael B. McDonald IV, "The Value of Middle Market Investment Bankers" (unpublished paper, September 2016).

- helping to prepare the company and management before approaching the market;
- maintaining transaction momentum—"time kills deals";
- enabling management to remain focused on the core business;
- allowing management to maintain an amicable relationship with the potential buyer, who may end up being their employer after the transaction; and
- limiting risk by facilitating more thorough due diligence.

These additional benefits should not be ignored. In most cases they are just as important, and in some cases, even more important, than the direct consideration received in a deal, especially for ESOP-owned companies.

The study of private equity firms referred to above found that private equity firms rated the extent that an investment banker makes the due diligence process run more smoothly for the seller and the buyer as an 8.1 out of 10.[3]

Potential buyers making unsolicited bids will often tell a company that if the company participates in an auction process, its offer is "off the table." My experience is that this is not the case. In fact, not only does the bidder participate in the process, they usually increase their bid as they learn more and get a sense that there is competition. When a potential buyer makes this kind of threat, you should step back and consider why the buyer is trying to create this sort of pressure. First, why do you think they do not want you to shop their offer? The potential buyer knows that if you go through a process you are likely to get a significantly better offer. Simply put, the buyer is trying to purchase the company at a discount to its true fair market value. Even if the offer price is at a significant premium to the annual valuation, that value may not include cost savings, revenue enhancements, and other strategic considerations (like the value to a potential buyer increasing market share, or just plain "fit"). If one bidder sees value at that price, others will usually also. Furthermore, although it may seem quicker and easier to deal with a single party, it usually turns out not to be

3. HighBank Advisors, "Selling Your Business."

the case. When a seller is dealing with a single buyer, that buyer has more leverage than they would have had in a competitive process. It is easier for that buyer to make demands on the seller, and such a buyer often "retrades" price and other terms after the seller is too far down the road to pursue other options.

Whether the ESOP is a minority or majority owner, the company's management, the board of directors, the ESOP trustee, and any other stakeholders (including warrant holders) should discuss an offer with an investment banking firm licensed by the Financial Industry Regulatory Authority (FINRA). Most of the time, the investment banking firm will meet with interested parties and provide a "free" assessment as part of its sales effort.

Case Study

Problem

The company started discussions with and received an unsolicited offer from a prospective buyer. The company and buyer agreed to a price (a 15% premium to valuation). After going through due diligence, the buyer and seller were not able to agree on sale terms since the buyer wanted indemnification provisions, a large escrow, and a large earnout.

Solution

Since word had already gotten out that the company was selling, management was concerned about employee morale and about losing customers to the competition. The board engaged an investment banking firm that ran a process looking for financial or strategic buyers. Strategic buyers felt that significant cost savings and revenue enhancements were available through a merger. Because the investment banker educated the potential buyers on specific issues related to purchasing an ESOP-owned company, the due diligence and negotiation went much smoother. The company wound up selling to a competitor, who agreed to a small escrow and no earnout. The total consideration exceeded the prior offer by 30% without regard to the earnout, and by 8% even assuming the full earnout was achieved.

Fiduciary Duties of the Board and Trustees

Under the Employee Retirement Income Security Act of 1974 (ERISA), an ERISA fiduciary, such as an ESOP trustee, must discharge their duties "solely in the interest of the participants and beneficiaries and . . .

with the care, skill, prudence, and diligence under the circumstances then prevailing that a prudent [person] acting in a like capacity and familiar with such matters would use in the conduct of an enterprise of a like character and with like aims."[4]

Boards of directors generally are not subject to ERISA's fiduciary duty requirements in relation to the ESOP other than in its selection of the trustee. Rather, boards are generally subject to the fiduciary duties of care and loyalty under state corporate law, which varies from state to state.[5] These fiduciary standards are distinct and different from the fiduciary standards of an ESOP trustee under ERISA. In the sale of a non-ESOP company, the board is usually advised to select a buyer based on a vibrant, competitive process to protect against breach of fiduciary claims. Often, boards are also advised to obtain an opinion directed to them that the consideration is fair from a financial perspective, which opinion is somewhat similar to the opinion given to the ESOP trustee (as discussed below), but often with more detail and complexity, and subject to retroactive scrutiny from FINRA.

The common process for the sale of an ESOP company is very different:

- Management receives an offer that is disclosed to the board, which then makes a determination that the offer should be pursued.
- Management, typically without the assistance of the ESOP trustee, then negotiates with the buyer to achieve what management believes is the best deal possible under the circumstances, taking into consideration the tax structure of the entities and the after-tax proceeds.
- The ESOP trustee then engages a "financial advisor," who updates the ESOP valuation and issues an opinion that the consideration received in the transaction is "adequate consideration" under ERISA Section 3(18) and that the terms of the transaction, taken

---

4. ERISA Section 404(a)(1)(B).

5. See "Fiduciary Issues and Practical Solutions for ESOP Company Boards When Responding to Acquisition Offers" in this book for an extensive discussion of the board's fiduciary duties under state law.

as a whole, are fair and reasonable to the ESOP from a financial point of view.

  - Since this opinion is directed to the ESOP trustee from an ERISA fiduciary perspective, it is not intended to provide evidence that the board has satisfied its fiduciary duties under state law.
  - Although the opinion addresses adequate consideration as defined in ERISA, this is not necessarily adequacy from a financial perspective in the context of a sale to a strategic buyer after taking into account strategic considerations (e.g., taking out a competitor) or cost savings and revenue enhancements.
  - The financial advisor explicitly states that it is not acting in a fiduciary capacity in reaching this opinion.

- The board then approves the transaction and related documentation (sometimes without the benefit of a price determined by a competitive process or an opinion directed to them that the consideration of the transaction is fair from a financial perspective) and directs that the transaction be submitted to the trustee and other shareholders.
- The trustee then relies on the non-fiduciary fairness opinion to determine that the transaction satisfies ERISA's fiduciary requirements to act solely in the interests of the participants and beneficiaries and either approves or rejects the transaction.

However, this type of process leaves critical questions unanswered. Would the ESOP's participants and beneficiaries, as well as the other relevant stakeholders, have received more consideration and/or better terms if the company and trustee had engaged an investment banker to run a professionally managed competitive sales process? To what extent can a director rely on the trustee's fairness opinion in connection with meeting their fiduciary duties?

In 2019, a former employee of an ESOP-owned company that was sold to a private equity firm filed a class action complaint alleging that, among other things, (1) the company's CEO and chair of the board of directors did not market the company to many potential buyers, including competitors, who would have paid more for the ESOP's shares;

and (2) in approving the purchase transaction, the ESOP trustee and the ESOP committee depended on a valuation that considered neither the characteristics of all of the potential buyers nor the price that those buyers would have paid for the shares.[6] Since filing this complaint, the class was certified on June 16, 2021, and various motions have been filed, but nothing else has been decided on its merits. These allegations could not have been made if they engaged an investment banker and ran a competitive sales process.

As discussed above, smart money private equity investors who regularly engage in buying and selling portfolio companies and are trying to achieve the highest possible returns almost always run a competitive sales process. If it is prudent for a private equity company to run a competitive process, why wouldn't management, the board of directors, the ESOP trustee, and any other stakeholders do the same to fulfill their duties?

Getting Free Advice

Although nothing in life is free, asking an investment banker to discuss a potential transaction may be about as close as it gets. Most investment bankers are eager to meet with companies that may be sold. In these meetings, the investment banker will discuss the typical transaction process. More importantly, if investment bankers are provided sufficient information in advance, they will also provide detailed feedback on where they believe the transaction will be valued in a competitive process and the likelihood of reaching a successful conclusion. Also, most investment banking fees are not only dependent on the price obtained but also contingent on a successful transaction. Therefore, if the fee is structured properly (as discussed below), then you will have a clear indication of the anticipated market value of the company.

The Competitive Process

During the initial phases of an engagement, an investment banker works to understand the importance of the following considerations:

6. Class Action Complaint, Rush v. GreatBanc Trust Company, No. 1:19-cv-00738 (N.D. Ill. Feb. 5, 2019), ECF No. 1.

- maximization of value and after-tax net proceeds
- financial and tax considerations
- transaction certainty and timing
- risk allocation for pre-closing acts or omissions discovered after closing
- desire of management to continue with the company after the transaction
- impact on other shareholders, family members, customers, suppliers, and/or creditors
- impact on management, employees, and communities
- different goals and objectives among other stakeholders
- protection of management and directors from post-closing liabilities to stakeholders in connection with pricing and other terms
- continuation of company name and corporate culture

Once the objectives and priorities are established, the investment banker tailors the process and the transaction structure to best address these considerations.

The typical process involves the investment banker performing some level of due diligence on both the company and the industry. Based on the results of that due diligence, the investment banker prepares "go-to-market" documents, including a "no-name" company summary, a confidentiality agreement, and a confidential information memorandum. The investment banker also researches and identifies potential buyers and/or investors. Working with the company, the investment banker will determine which potential buyers and investors to contact. A quality investment banker, working with the owner, management, and legal advisors, will also prepare an online data room and populate it with appropriate files.

Case Study

Problem

A direct competitor approached the company's president about buying the company. The buyer wanted to sign a letter of intent that would provide it with a 90-day exclusivity period, financing, and due diligence outs, and said it would pay a 10% premium to the company's prior valuation.

Solution

The company's board of directors was concerned that this buyer might not be capable of consummating the transaction. The board asked an investment banking firm to present alternatives to selling to this buyer. The investment banker explained that before going exclusive and providing full access to the company's books and records, they should first receive a source-of-funds statement from the buyer. The buyer disclosed that it was planning to 100% bank finance the transaction. The company and the investment banker both agreed that receiving 100% bank financing was not likely. Also, the investment banker felt that they could do better in a competitive process. The company engaged the investment banker to run a process. The investment banker received 11 indications of interest, invited 6 in for management meetings, and received 3 offers, all above the unsolicited bid and all with sufficient financing. The company ultimately accepted an offer and closed an all-cash transaction at a price that 18% higher than the unsolicited offer.

When it is time to go to market, the investment banker will contact prospects on a "no-name" basis. To the extent that prospects show interest based on the summary "no-name" information and before receiving any confidential information, the prospects sign a confidentiality agreement. Once the confidentiality agreement is in place, the investment banker distributes the confidential information memorandum to potential buyers. After reviewing the confidential information memorandum and having a chance to discuss the company with the investment banker, the prospects are asked to submit preliminary or first-round bids. To the extent there are discrepancies, the banker will work with the prospect to make sure that all of the bids are made on terms that can be accurately compared and contrasted. The banker will then review first-round bids with the trustee, other stakeholders, and management to select which prospects should have access to a data room, meet with management, and participate in facility tours. After such access, management presentations, and tours, the banker will solicit and negotiate second-round bids.

To facilitate a purchase agreement that can be "bidded" as part of the competitive process, many bankers will work with company counsel to draft a term sheet or purchase agreement and ask remaining bidders to comment on the document before picking a winner. As bidders go through their due diligence process, the banker will work with management to answer questions from and additional due diligence requests of bidders. After questions have been answered, the bidders will be asked to submit a final-round bid, letters of intent (typically binding the bidder to purchase the company with as few "outs" as possible) and a "mark-up" of the transaction agreements. The investment banker works with the trustee, stakeholders, and management to choose a bidder to move to the final phase. The process is always fluid, sometimes requiring fewer and sometimes more "rounds" of bidding, sometimes moving more quickly to negotiating with a single party, but almost always with the attempt to keep it competitive as long as possible.

In the final phase, the investment banker leads the negotiation of the "business" and "economic" issues in the transaction documents. The investment banker attempts to maximize after-tax net proceeds, minimize escrows and indemnity exposure, and maximize transaction certainty. The investment banker will interface with the company's other advisors (lawyers, accountants, trustees, etc.) to make sure that the process goes as smoothly as possible. Most importantly, the investment banker should be maintaining transaction momentum and sense of urgency until close.

Table 3-1 provides an overview of the typical phases of an investment banker engagement.

Typical Engagement Timeline and Fees

Although every engagement is different and presents unique and often unanticipated challenges, it is always a long, complex process. If everything goes according to plan, the process takes around six months. However, even the insertion of the most seemingly innocuous event can add months to the timeline. A good investment banker will attempt to maintain deal momentum throughout the process, even when unexpected delays occur. See figure 3-1 for an illustration of a timeline.

Most bankers work primarily on a contingent fee basis. There is typically a retainer fee that is paid up front. This fee is charged to make sure that the client is committed to the process and is not just shopping to see what the company is worth. Although the upfront retainer is a small percentage of the total fee, it needs to be enough

Table 3-1. Overview of typical phases of an engagement

Evaluation	Preparation	Solicitation	Negotiation	Finalization
• Determine stakeholder objectives and priorities – Economic – Family – Management – Continued involvement – Company name and culture – Community • Perform preliminary analysis of company and industry • Research market environment • Negotiate and sign engagement agreement with trustee, stakeholders, and company	• Perform company and industry due diligence • Prepare documents to "go to market" – "No-name" company summary – Confidentiality agreement – Memorandum • Research and identify potential buyers/investors • Determine potential buyers/investors to contact • Prepare buyer/investor data room files	• Contact potential buyers/investors on a "no-name" basis • Sign confidentiality agreements with potential buyers/investors • Distribute memorandum to potential buyers • Solicit and negotiate first-round bids • Review potential buyers/investors with trustee, stakeholders, and company to select potential buyers/investors to meet with management and participate in facility tours • Hold management presentations/tours • Solicit and negotiate second-round bids	• Provide data room files to remaining potential buyers/investors • Distribute draft purchase agreement to remaining potential buyers • Address due diligence questions and requests • Solicit and negotiate third-round bids/letters of intent and "mark-ups" to the transaction agreement (additional bid rounds may be required or desired depending on the process) • Work with trustee, stakeholders, and company to choose a potential buyer/investor to move to the final phase	• Lead negotiation of the "business" and "economic" issues in the transaction documents • Maximize after-tax net proceeds • Minimize escrows and indemnity exposure • Interface with client's other advisors – Legal – Accounting/tax – Trustee • Coordinate and manage final buyer/investor due diligence • Maintain transaction momentum and sense of urgency until close

In each phase, the client has the opportunity to control the direction of the process.

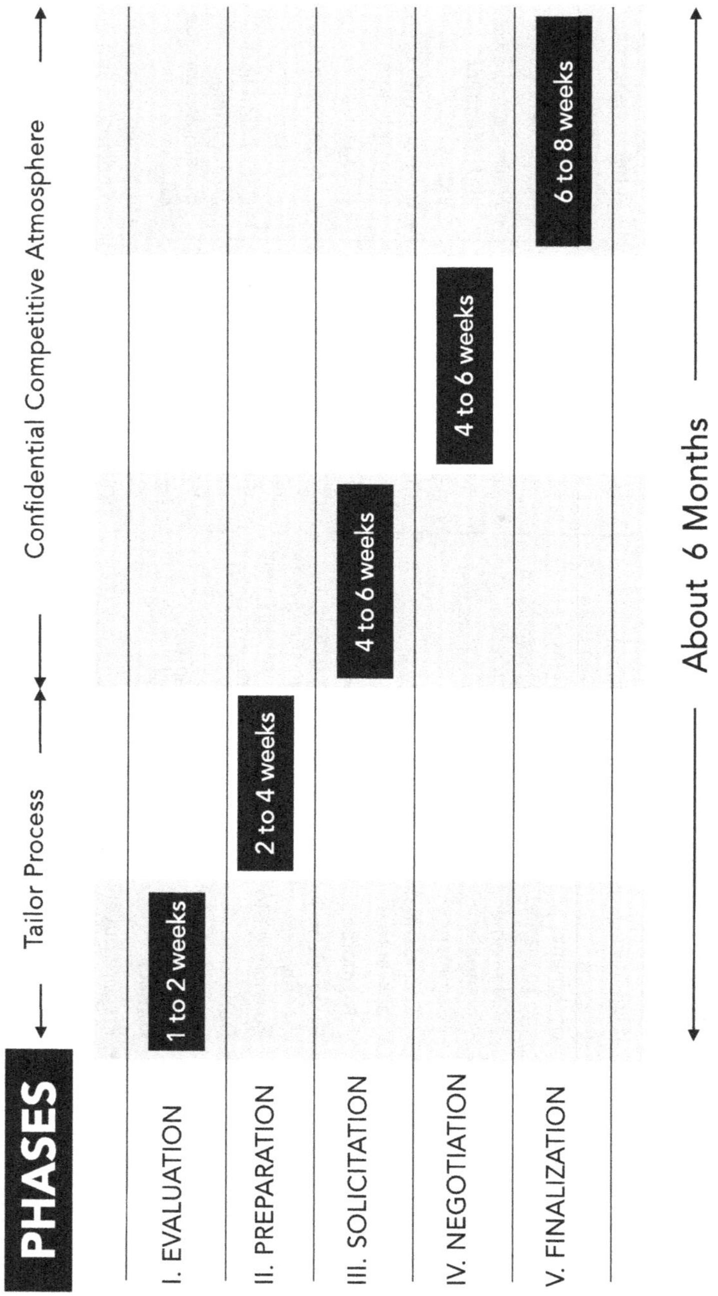

Figure 3-1. Typical engagement timeline

to make sure that the client is committed and that the interests of the company and the investment banker are aligned (i.e., both parties need to have "skin in the game").

The bulk of the fee is usually variable and based on the sale price of the company. Although there are different formulas used by different investment bankers, one method that works well and aligns the interest of the stakeholders and the investment banker is called a Reverse Lehman formula. The Reverse Lehman formula calls for the fee to be based on one percentage of enterprise value up to a base value (which is mutually agreed upon by the banker and the company, often based on the value received in an unsolicited offer). A higher percentage is applied to the enterprise value over that base value. This type of fee better aligns the interest of the banker and the stakeholders to achieve the maximum transaction value.

Advantages of Dealing with a Licensed Investment Banking Firm

With few exceptions, only firms licensed under state or federal statutes can act as a company's representative and legally collect a commission or success fee for helping sell a company. The gold standard is investment bankers licensed as broker-dealers by FINRA. FINRA regularly examines all licensed firms to determine compliance with FINRA's rules and those of the SEC and the Municipal Securities Rulemaking Board (MSRB). FINRA evaluates a firm's supervisory system and determines whether adequate financial and operational systems are in place. It also requires individual licensees to pass qualification exams to demonstrate competence in their particular activities. FINRA, in conjunction with other self-regulatory organizations and the Securities Industry/Regulatory Council on Continuing Education, administers the continuing education program for the securities industry. FINRA operates a central licensing and registration system that provides the qualification, employment, and disclosure histories of active registered individuals. Finally, FINRA provides a formal process to determine and enforce breaches of regulatory or ethical rules and provides transparency for such matters.

Business brokers are not subject to examination, supervision, continuing education, and other regulations of FINRA. Most business brokers also do not have the same research and analysis capabilities or access to investors, and they typically do not conduct the same rigorous process as do investment bankers.

Closing Thoughts

Selling a business is not like selling a house. There is no Multiple Listing Service. Usually, there are no readily available reliable "comparables." One cannot simply put a sign in one's yard and wait for offers to follow. In addition to maximizing sales proceeds, the seller should be concerned about minimizing legal liability, maintaining confidentiality, maintaining deal momentum, and otherwise minimizing execution risk. These concerns need to be addressed throughout the sales process, while at the same time management needs to stay focused on running the business.

These issues are exacerbated when a company is ESOP-owned. In addition to dealing with all of the normal concerns of selling a business, advisors also need to understand the intricacies of unallocated shares, ESOP leverage, when participant pass-through voting is required, and receiving not just board approval but also approval of the ESOP trustee. The board and trustee have the additional concern of participating in a transaction and fulfilling their fiduciary duties, both to the company and its stakeholders, while also following ERISA and state laws. By running a professionally managed, vibrant process with a licensed investment banker who has ESOP expertise, all parties can be assured that they have done everything possible to maximize value for those stakeholders.

4

Operational Issues Stemming from the Sale of an ESOP Company

Nancy Dittmer

THIS CHAPTER DISCUSSES the operational issues that arise when an ESOP company is sold. It does not discuss the fiduciary and legal issues relating to the analysis of the offer, the negotiation process, or any of the other steps leading up to the actual transaction, which are discussed elsewhere in this book. Rather, it starts with the assumption that the offer has been accepted. Based on that assumption, what happens to the ESOP?

The sale can be structured as either a stock sale or an asset sale. In a stock sale, the shares allocated to the participants' accounts will generally be sold to the third-party buyer as a part of the transaction. If the transaction is an asset sale, then the ESOP sponsor will receive cash for the sale of its assets, and the ESOP will receive its appropriate share of this cash when the corporation is dissolved. An asset sale requires a pass-through vote to the participants to approve or disapprove of the sale.

In either type of sale, the ESOP's investment in stock is eventually liquidated into cash and/or other marketable securities.

If the ESOP is leveraged, then one of the first questions is what will happen to the outstanding loan balance. This should be a point of negotiation with the trustee of the ESOP before the offer is finalized and accepted. The trustee may negotiate for the repayment of the loan in advance of the transaction. Of course, any payments on the debt, whether through contributions, dividends, or redemptions must comply with the Internal Revenue Code and the Employee Retirement Income Security Act (ERISA). This may limit the ability to repay the debt before the transaction.

In many cases, the shares held in the loan suspense account will be sold as a part of the transaction. If the sales proceeds exceed the outstanding loan balance, then the excess must be allocated among participants' accounts. The ESOP document will likely need to be amended to indicate the methodology for such allocation of the excess. For example, will the allocation of the excess be made pro rata based on compensation or pro rata based on share account balances?

If the stock held as collateral is worth less than the face amount of the debt, it can frequently be canceled under the employer's guarantee.

There should be consultation with advisors on all of these issues relating to the ESOP's outstanding loan.

In many transactions, the buyer wishes to structure the transaction to include some type of escrow account or earnout payments. Certain types of contingent payments may be considered prohibited transactions if received by the ESOP, so consultation with legal counsel will be needed during the negotiation stage. Assuming that the deferred payment to the ESOP is permitted, then the ESOP could be retained until all such future payments are received. This would require the continuation of annual allocations, reporting to the participants, and Form 5500 preparation, as well as amendments to the plan document as needed for legislative or regulatory activity. (Note: if the company stock has been liquidated, there would not be a requirement for an independent valuation.)

Once these issues are resolved and the ESOP's investment in company stock has been converted into cash or marketable securities, what happens to the participants' balances in the ESOP? Whether the ESOP will be continued by the successor, terminated by the successor, or terminated before the acquisition will also be determined during the negotiation process. In most transactions, the ESOP will be terminated as a part of the transaction. It may be possible to merge the ESOP into a plan maintained by the buyer, but that does not occur frequently due to liability concerns on the part of the buyer. In other words, any qualification issues pertaining to the ESOP may be carried over to the buyer's plan as a part of such merger. Also, there may be a need to maintain certain protected benefits and rights of the ESOP in the buyer's plan, and that may not be desirable. For these reasons, the ESOP is often terminated.

The termination of an ESOP is not unlike the termination of any other qualified retirement plan in that the end result is that each participant receives a distribution of the balance in their account. However, there are many issues to be considered to get to the end result. The board of directors will adopt a resolution to terminate the plan and specify the termination date and other pertinent facts.

The ESOP document may need to be amended to address issues relating to the plan termination. For example, the company may make a final contribution, but this contribution may be for a period of less than a plan year. So the document may need to be amended to specify how this contribution will be allocated (e.g., defining the short-period compensation and the hours of service to be considered.) The document may also need to be amended to address the payouts to ESOP participants. For example, if the ESOP document currently provides for installment distributions, the ESOP may be amended to now allow for lump-sum distributions. The document may need to be amended to allow for partial distributions while awaiting a determination letter from the IRS. The document may also need to be amended to eliminate the distribution in the form of company stock, assuming that eliminating it is permissible (the elimination of the right to demand company stock is permissible to the extent that the company stock has been sold to a third-party buyer). Finally, there may also be amendments required to bring the ESOP document into compliance with all recent legislative and regulatory updates.

The termination of the ESOP does trigger 100% vesting for all participants remaining in the ESOP at the time of the termination. The 100% vesting will apply to any current employee as well as any former employee with a balance remaining in the ESOP who has not yet incurred a forfeiture event (e.g., five consecutive one-year breaks in service).

The plan sponsor must decide whether to file for an IRS determination letter with respect to the termination of the ESOP. The applicable filing is Form 5310, Application for Determination Upon Termination. Filing Form 5310 is not required. The purpose of filing Form 5310 is to obtain assurance from the IRS that the ESOP was qualified at the time of termination so as to avoid a qualification defect being raised in a future IRS audit that would require some type of correction. The Form 5310 asks for information relating to the operation of the ESOP in the years before the termination. Again, an ESOP sponsor should consult with its advisors on whether the Form 5310 should be filed.

If the decision is made to file the Form 5310, the next decision is whether to postpone all or at least some of the distributions to the participants until the IRS issues its determination letter. If all of the assets are distributed immediately and the IRS does find a qualification defect, the available correction alternatives are limited. Therefore, it may be prudent to postpone the distribution of at least some portion of the balances until the IRS issues its determination letter. That process could take six to nine months or longer.

If the time to obtain an IRS determination letter crosses the end of a plan year, then there will be a need for allocations of earnings, preparation of participant statements, and Form 5500 filing, including audited financial statements if applicable, for such plan year.

Once the ESOP investments are liquid and/or the IRS determination letter has been received, the next steps are to distribute the balances to the participants. Each participant will have the election to make a direct rollover of the distribution into another qualified retirement plan or an Individual Retirement Account (IRA) or to take the distribution directly net of applicable income tax withholding.

If the plan administrator is unable to locate all participants or cannot obtain signed election forms from all participants, then IRA accounts may need to be established for such participants.

There will likely be the need for a final earnings allocation before the final distributions are made. Once all distributions have been processed, the final Form 5500 can be prepared.

As outlined above, this process may take a year or more, so a critical item to keep in mind is that someone must remain responsible for the completion of this process. Where the plan sponsor has ceased to exist as part of a business transaction, the original documents should include stipulations as to who will be responsible for the closing of the ESOP, signing returns, responding to IRS or DOL inquiries, etc.

This chapter may make this process sound burdensome, but the key point to remember is that with the liquidation of the ESOP comes the financial delivery of those ownership benefits to the plan participants. That justifies all of the steps that must be taken to get there.

5

Sale of an ESOP Sponsor Company: Questions of Time, Money, People, and the Law

Randolph R. Smith, Jr.

WHEN CLOSELY HELD BUSINESS OWNERS sell their stock to an ESOP, they may believe this will be their last corporate transaction. Often, however, and particularly with successful ESOP companies, potential buyers come calling. This chapter explores the processes by which closely held ESOP companies manage a possible sale to a third party, including the roles of the board, the ESOP trustee and company management. It also considers what documents may be involved in such a sale, including the fairness opinion provided by the ESOP's independent financial advisor. This discussion assumes that the ESOP was initially financed with seller financing, but most of what is described here would apply no matter how the sale was financed.

First Steps When an Offer Comes In

Role of the President

You sold your closely held company to an ESOP. Then a strategic buyer with what appears to be an attractive offer calls. What do you do next?

The president or other officer of the ESOP sponsor company (the "sponsor company") often is the first to receive an offer from a strategic buyer (the "buyer"). The president may also (1) be a member of the board of directors, (2) hold a seller note from when he or she sold his or her shares to the ESOP, and/or (3) hold warrants attached to the seller note. And, in fact, the president may be the ESOP trustee (the "ESOP trustee" or "trustee") because the sponsor company may have transitioned from an independent trustee to an insider trustee after the ESOP stock purchase closed.

When an officer has so many different roles and responsibilities, the purchase offer creates a conflict of interest. Therefore, the officer is left wondering, when evaluating the offer, in what role he or she should act and how to avoid a breach of fiduciary duty lawsuit.

The president first evaluates the offer in his or her role as an officer of the sponsor company in order to evaluate whether or not the offer is legitimate and may, in fact, be a bona fide offer. If the officer determines that the offer is legitimate and may be in the interest of the employer corporation and shareholders, then the officer should present the offer to the board of directors.

The Role of the Board

The officers and the board avoid a breach of fiduciary duty by observing procedural prudence in their review of the offer. This means they should establish a reasonable process for evaluating offers and document their activities as they proceed. If, for example, the board's decision is challenged and a court determines that the board has followed procedural prudence (thereby preserving the business judgment rule), the court will evaluate the decision-making process, not the actual decision. This will work heavily in the board's favor.

The board should be adequately informed about the economic and legal ramifications of selling the sponsor company. It should seek counsel from qualified advisors about the ramifications of a sale. For example, under Internal Revenue Code ("Code") Section 4978, if (1) the shareholder who sold to the ESOP took Section 1042 treatment on the proceeds in order to defer capital gains tax and (2) the ESOP sells its shares within three years of the ESOP's purchase of the shares, then the sponsor company must pay a 10% excise tax on the amount realized on the sale. There are, however, exceptions to this rule, such as a sale to satisfy normal plan distribution requirements, and a stock-for-stock exchange in a tax-free reorganization with another company.

Next, the board must perform preliminary due diligence to determine whether the offer is a bona fide offer, which means that (1) the offer was made in good faith and (2) the buyer can pay for it (i.e., the buyer has cash or financing).

At this stage, what kind of due diligence does the board perform—financial, legal, or both? The board (or a committee of the board) first typically performs general financial due diligence on the buyer and meets with the buyer's executives (1) to discuss the two companies' business strategies, vision, and goals, and (2) to evaluate mutual interests. The parties usually share financial and other data.

The seller, however, should beware that the buyer may be on a fishing expedition—for example, to learn about the sponsor company's technology or proprietary processes. Therefore, before the parties exchange information, it is prudent to sign a confidentiality agreement.

The Role of the Trustee

If the ESOP trustee is an inside trustee, the trustee will likely not only be aware of what is happening but also participate in the discussions. At this point, the trustee should participate only in the capacity of an officer or director and not in his or her capacity as trustee. If the ESOP trustee is an outside trustee, it is good practice to inform the trustee that the sponsor company has been approached by a potential buyer. Once the board determines that the offer is bona fide and approves the offer, however, it must inform the ESOP trustee of the offer. The trustee then comes to the bargaining table.

If there has been an inside trustee up to that point, the inside trustee should resign, and the board should appoint an independent outside discretionary trustee to evaluate the transaction and to serve as the ESOP trustee for the deal.

An ESOP attorney, the ESOP valuation advisor, or the NCEO are often good referral sources for an independent trustee. ESOP sponsor companies that already have an independent trustee may choose to make the ESOP trustee aware of the offer early in the process so that the trustee is not surprised. Early awareness and open communication could enable the ESOP trustee to move faster to the next stage.

Even in a 100% ESOP-owned sponsor company, the ESOP trustee will recognize that the initial evaluation of an offer is a board function. Therefore, while from a fiduciary standpoint the ESOP trustee is not required to be involved with the initial evaluation of the offer, the board might choose to keep the ESOP trustee informed if it appears to the board that the offer will move to the next stage. The next stage is typically the letter of intent stage.

Buyers unaccustomed to ESOP sponsor companies are often confused when the independent trustee arrives at the bargaining table. This is because, to date, the buyer has dealt with, for example, the company's president, who sold his or her shares to the ESOP in exchange for (1) a seller note possibly secured by the company's assets and/or a pledge of the ESOP shares and (2) seller financing warrants for sponsor company stock. The president may also have been acting as the inside trustee. Therefore, the uninformed buyer may think that the president controls the company and the ESOP. And the uninformed buyer may bargain accordingly and ignore the ESOP's interests.

Going into the letter of intent stage, it is important for the buyer to understand that the ESOP is a separate party to the deal. This fact may not be obvious, particularly if the ESOP is relatively new and a substantial portion of the shares has not been allocated to the ESOP participant accounts. Legally, however, the ESOP trustee is the record owner of all allocated and unallocated shares.

If there is a seller note outstanding, effectively, there will be two simultaneous acquisitions:

1. A note acquisition between the buyer and the seller note holder who, as the sponsor company's creditor, possibly holds a security interest in the assets of the company, which could include a pledge of the unallocated shares owned by the ESOP.
2. A stock acquisition between the buyer and the ESOP trustee, as the legal owner of the shares.

While a letter of intent is not required, parties typically enter into them. Note, however, that ESOP trustees typically do not want to sign a letter of intent, particularly if the sale is structured as an asset sale. This is because in an asset sale, the sponsor company—not the ESOP trustee—is actually the seller. If it is a stock sale, the ESOP trustee most often signs the letter of intent because legally the ESOP trustee owns the shares. Even if the purchase is an asset deal, the ESOP trustee will need to approve the letter of intent.

After the board appoints the independent ESOP trustee, the trustee hires a valuation advisor and an attorney. The sponsor company's attorney will want to review and comment on the engagement letters of the ESOP trustee's valuation advisor and the ESOP trustee's attorney.

It is an unusual aspect of the ESOP structure that, while the ESOP trustee and its team must remain independent of the company and the seller note holder, the sponsor company often pays the fees of the ESOP trustee and its professional advisors. Therefore, the sponsor company will be a signatory to those engagement letters for purposes of paying the fees. Even if the company and the seller note holder want the ESOP to pay the fees of the professionals who advise the ESOP, the law limits the kinds of fees that the ESOP can pay. The ESOP can pay fees for certain typical deal-related actions, such as the negotiation, documentation, and coordination of the purchase of the ESOP's shares.

The ESOP cannot, however, pay the fees for what are referred to as "settlor" functions. These functions can include the correction of any operational failures from the ESOP's annual employer administration The sponsor company, not the ESOP, must pay those fees. ESOP counsel typically helps the ESOP trustee navigate fee and conflict issues.

Sale Structure, Letters of Intent, and Exclusivity Agreements

Purchases of ESOP sponsor companies are often structured as stock sales. This is because if, for example, the ESOP sponsor company is a C corporation there could be a double tax—once at the corporate level and once at the personal level. Furthermore, if the sale is structured as a sale of substantially all of the sponsor company's assets (or a merger, or involves a recapitalization, dissolution, or liquidation), the Code, together with applicable state law, could require "pass-through voting" by ESOP participants.

With pass-through voting, the ESOP participants must instruct the trustee as to how the shares allocated to their accounts are to be voted (the ESOP trustee still votes the unallocated shares). This can increase the expense and time involved in the transaction. In a stock sale, however, the ESOP trustee typically votes for or against the transaction on behalf of the participants, which the parties see as being more cost- and time-efficient.[1]

The letter of intent often sets out the time frame in two phases:

1. Phase one may be a 30-day, nonexclusive phase in which (a) the parties exchange financial information, (b) management meets to discuss in detail the post-transaction picture, and (c) the ESOP trustee's financial advisor does a preliminary review of the fairness of the proposed transaction to the ESOP from a financial point of view. This review includes a study of relative fairness (i.e., a comparison of what the ESOP will get to what any other sellers and/or company executives will get).
2. Phase 2 is often a 60-day exclusivity period, during which the parties engage in (a) detailed legal due diligence, (b) detailed financial due diligence, and possibly (c) a site visit at the seller company. with the buyer's management.

Typical provisions that are at issue in the letters of intent include the following:

- adjustments to the purchase price
- taxes
- indemnification
- consideration (cash versus stock)
- time frame

It is helpful to resolve material issues early. However, except for limited provisions (e.g., confidentiality, exclusivity, and a trustee "fiduciary out"), the letter of intent is usually nonbinding.

---

1. Note that the ESOP plan document might grant pass-through voting rights in the case of a stock sale, or the ESOP trustee can ask the ESOP participants to vote on a stock sale.

Letters of intent typically make the deal closing contingent on the completion of certain events:

- completion of due diligence satisfactory to the buyer and the seller
- settlement of accounts receivables, notes receivables, accounts payable, distributions payable, and notes payable among related parties
- the sponsor company conducting business in the ordinary course until closing with no material adverse change in business
- approval by the buyer's board
- execution of a definitive purchase agreement and related agreements, such as a shareholders' agreement of the acquiring entity if the buyer's stock is consideration

The letter of intent usually states an enterprise value, which is subject to decrease by the amount of third-party debt, notes payable, capital leases, prepayment penalties, debt retirement costs, and other adjustments. The closing will also be contingent on the ESOP trustee receiving a favorable fairness opinion from its financial advisor.

Because the ESOP trustee has not had, and will not have, operational control over the sponsor company, the trustee typically will not want to agree to adjustments to the purchase price for working capital or taxes, and the ESOP trustee will not agree to indemnify the buyer. The buyer typically has to look to the seller note holder or other selling shareholders for any such adjustments and recourse. If the buyer's stock is consideration, the ESOP trustee typically will not agree to enter into a shareholders' agreement if the agreement contains drag-along or similar provisions under which the ESOP would be required to sell, or not to sell, its shares. This is because such provisions are contrary to the ESOP trustee's fiduciary duty under ERISA to act solely in the interest of the ESOP participants.

There may be pressure for the parties to sign the letter of intent with provisions that the parties would not agree to in the purchase agreement. The argument for this is that the letter of intent is nonbinding, and the parties need to move on to get a deal done. This often simply delays arguments over issues.

While it is true that most of the provisions in the letter of intent are not be binding, it may put the sellers in a poor bargaining position because it creates the perception that the parties have reached an agreement.

Just before the non-exclusivity phase ends, the sponsor company and the buyer may want an oral approval from the ESOP trustee and the ESOP trustee's financial advisor that the deal terms are fair to the ESOP from a financial point of view. The motivation for this is to get an indication that there is, in fact, a deal (i.e., a meeting of the minds) before the parties spend the money to do in-depth legal and financial due diligence.

If the deal consideration is cash only (even if the payment of a portion is subject to escrows and/ or earnouts), it is a relatively easy exercise for the ESOP trustee's financial advisor to determine whether the proposed transaction is fair to the ESOP from a financial point of view. If, however, the consideration is stock in the buyer corporation, or a mix of cash and stock in the buyer corporation, there are usually so many unanswered questions before the in-depth legal and financial analysis stage that it may not be possible for the ESOP trustee's financial advisor to make a judgment at that point. In such a case, the financial advisor may give an oral indication that the consideration offered is within a reasonable range, but with many caveats.

Upon signing the letter of intent, the sponsor company typically adopts an "iron curtain amendment" to the ESOP plan document, whereby diversification and distributions to participants are suspended until after the date on which the transaction closes or is terminated because the consideration that the ESOP would receive in the transaction would likely be greater than the value of the sponsor company stock as of the plan year-end.

Cash, Stock, or Both?

If stock, or a mix of cash and stock, is offered to the ESOP as consideration, the ESOP trustee's financial advisor will not only have to value the sponsor company, it will have to value the buyer corporation, which is impossible to do until complete financial and legal due diligence is performed on the buyer. As a result, there can be a circular dilemma.

This is because the buyer will want the ESOP trustee to agree to the consideration offered. But, it is not possible to agree until the ESOP trustee's valuation advisor and legal advisor have completed their work. The value proposition in buyer corporation stock may not be knowable at this point. For cost and timing reasons, it is helpful for the ESOP trustee and its financial advisor to determine sooner rather than later whether stock in the buyer corporation is desirable.

If the ESOP trustee has the option to choose between cash or stock or a mix, if stock in the buyer corporation is at all compelling (which it may well be if the trustee believes there will be an immediate increase in value post-closing from the combined companies), there may be a strong financial case for taking all stock. An ESOP trustee may, however, take the view that giving up its relatively secure investment in the sponsor company's stock in exchange for stock in the buyer corporation is too risky. This could be because, for example, there is a fiduciary concern in giving up shares in a solid company that is known to the trustee and that has good prospects for shares in a new, relatively unknown company, and in possibly trading a majority interest for a minority interest.

Often the seller note holder is in a better position to deal with the risk of taking stock in the buyer corporation. This is because he or she will go on to work at, and possibly have some operational control of, the buyer. Therefore, the ESOP trustee may rather choose to take a cash premium for the ESOP's shares.

The buyer also may come to realize that it does not really want the ESOP or the ESOP participants as shareholders. Other considerations are often used as "sweeteners" to the ESOP, such as rights in an earnout, rights in amounts in escrow, or guaranteed 401(k) contributions to former ESOP participants with immediate vesting.

The ESOP trustee's financial advisor, however, typically does not assign any value to these sweeteners in its fairness opinion analysis because the interests are considered to be too contingent and remote, which is a point that should be explained to the proposed buyer early in the process.

It is noteworthy that if the ESOP will continue to exist post-closing, in order for the ESOP to take the buyer's corporate stock, the stock must be "qualified employer securities" under Code Sections 4975(e)(8) and 409(l) and Treasury Regulation Section 54.495-12. This is because an ESOP can only invest in "qualified employer securities." This is not the case if the ESOP will be terminated. Qualified employer securities are defined as stock issued by the employer (or by a sponsor company that is of the same controlled group) that has a combination of voting and dividend rights equal to or greater than the class of stock of the employer (or of any company that is a member of the same controlled group) that has the greatest voting and dividend rights.

Because of the unique requirements of the ESOP trustee as seller, the ESOP stock is sometimes redeemed by the sponsor company for a cash premium immediately before other shareholders of the sponsor company sell their shares to the buyer.

The Fairness Opinion

The ESOP trustee's financial advisor will determine:

1. whether or not the consideration to be paid to the ESOP for its shares is equal to or greater than the fair market value of such shares (as such term is used in determining "adequate consideration" under Section 3(18) of ERISA); and
2. whether the transaction is fair to the ESOP from a financial point of view.

The fairness determination includes an analysis of the deal's relative fairness (e.g., is the ESOP getting as good a deal as the seller note holder or any other selling shareholder or manager?). The ESOP trustee's financial advisor will use as a benchmark for its analysis the financial position of the ESOP seven to ten years out, assuming that:

1. the company is not purchased;
2. all allocations are made;
3. all participants vest in their shares; and
4. the company meets its projections.[2]

---

2. There is no rule regarding the use of seven to ten years, but that time frame is often used because it is seen as a reasonable time period. Some valuation advi-

If the ESOP company is an S corporation, the financial advisor may include in its analysis the value of future S corporation tax deferrals. The ESOP trustee's financial advisor will then compare this benchmark position to the ESOP's financial position if the ESOP were to take cash in exchange for its shares. Or, if buyer corporation stock is a possibility, then it will compare the benchmark to the projected financial position of the ESOP seven to ten years out if the ESOP were to take stock in the buyer corporation.

The financial advisor will also compare the ESOP's possible financial positions to the financial position of any other selling parties, such as the seller note holder, to determine the relative fairness of the transaction.

From a fiduciary perspective, the ESOP trustee:

1. can only consider the net sale proceeds of the transaction; and
2. can only consider the financial aspects of the offer, not what might happen, for example, to the employees.

The fairness opinion must be dated as of the transaction closing date. The parties need to keep this in mind, particularly when the ESOP trustee is asked early in the process to give an oral indication that he or she agrees to the price because if there are significant delays during which time the sponsor company's performance improves, the price that was fair months before may not be fair on the closing date. In any case, the ESOP trustee cannot close without a favorable fairness opinion from its financial advisor.[3]

---

sors might choose to use the term of the ESOP loan instead, but, for example, it may not be practical to try to project forward more than ten years.

3. DOL guidance from the *Johnson v. Couturier* case (DOL Settlement: Civil Action No. 2:08-cv-02732-RRB-GGH) states that an ESOP trustee must make certain that reliance on the financial advisor's opinion is reasonably justified under the circumstances. The ESOP trustee cannot rely on the financial advisor's views unless the ESOP trustee has read and understands the valuation report and fairness opinion and any other supporting documents. The ESOP trustee (1) must have identified, questioned, and tested the financial data and underlying assumptions and (2) must have verified that the conclusions are consistent with the data and analyses and that the valuation report, fairness opinion, or any other requested report or advice is internally consistent and makes sense.

Price Protection

If the ESOP trustee determines that it wants the buyer's stock as consideration, it is important that the ESOP receive contractual "price protection" for the shares. This is because, for example, the ESOP may be trading a majority interest in the company for a minority interest in the buyer. Minority interests are typically subject to a discount in value of up to 30%. The possible result is, therefore, that immediately after the transaction, without price protection, the value of the ESOP's shares of the buyer corporation could decrease by up to 30%.

If the ESOP holds a majority of the sponsor company's stock and it cannot successfully obtain price protection in the buyer's stock, then the ESOP may require additional stock or cash to make up for that significant discount. The ESOP trustee will argue that price protection will not have a material impact on the buyer. This is because the failure to apply a minority discount is not likely to materially increase the buyer's repurchase obligation.

For example, if the buyer has a $200,000 repurchase obligation, with a minority discount of 20% that goes unapplied, that would only translate to an additional $40,000 of repurchase obligation, which is probably not going to be material to the buyer. On the other hand, a participant who has been terminated will likely view the portion of that $40,000 that he or she would have received had there been price protection as a material amount.

The buyer's articles of incorporation could be amended to state that any stock held by, or distributed by, the ESOP will not be subject to a discount for lack of control.

Key Aspects of the Purchase Agreement for the ESOP

With respect to the purchase agreement, the ESOP trustee typically will not agree to any indemnification provisions. Also, the ESOP trustee typically will only give limited representations and warranties (e.g., that it has the power to enter into the agreement and that it has title to the sponsor company stock). This procedure makes sense when one considers that the ESOP has not had and will not have operational control over the sponsor company.

Instead, the buyer typically looks to the seller note holder or other selling shareholders for any such provisions. Another option, particularly if the ESOP is the only seller, is for the sponsor company to make the representations and warranties and for the indemnification provisions to be backed up by representation and warranty insurance. It is important to make an uninformed buyer aware early in the transaction that this is the customary position of an ESOP regarding indemnification provisions, representations, and warranties so that there is plenty of time to obtain suitable representation and warranty insurance, the cost of which the buyer often covers, or which the sponsor company and the buyer sometimes split.

If the ESOP trustee will take stock in the buyer corporation, the ESOP trustee will want lengthy representations and warranties from the buyer, which can include the following:

- provisions regarding capitalization
- clear title to the buyer stock
- no outstanding litigation
- validity of financial statements
- no material adverse changes
- no unresolved environmental matters
- no unresolved taxation issues

In this way, the buyer is on the hook for indemnification to the ESOP trustee for a breach of any representation or warranty under the purchase agreement that adversely affects the value of the buyer corporation stock.

The ESOP trustee will usually want to make clear in the purchase agreement that the value of its consideration is not subject to any of the following:

- working capital adjustments
- adjustments for taxes
- third-party debt
- notes payable

- capital leases
- prepayment penalties
- debt retirement costs
- other adjustments

Rather, the buyer typically looks to the seller note holder or other selling shareholders for any such adjustments.

The purchase agreement will direct the flow of the consideration so that, for example, at closing the sponsor company can assign to the seller noteholder all of the sponsor company's rights in the ESOP note and pledge of ESOP shares. This assignment will constitute payment in full under the seller note. This will cause the seller note holder to cancel the seller note and any security agreement related thereto.

The ESOP can then assign to the seller note holder all of the unallocated shares. In exchange, the seller note holder can assign the ESOP note and pledge of ESOP shares to the ESOP trustee. This assignment will immediately cancel the ESOP note and the pledge of ESOP shares. After this, the unallocated shares will be unencumbered. The ESOP can then assign all of the allocated shares to the buyer in exchange for stock, cash, and/or other consideration. Finally, the seller note holder can assign to the buyer all of the unallocated shares in exchange for (1) a note (possibly with terms more favorable than the seller note), (2) stock, (3) cash, and/or (4) other consideration, subject to any closing or post-closing adjustments.

What Happens to the ESOP?

These are the options regarding the disposition of the ESOP that the parties typically consider upon a sale:

1. Terminate it and transfer the ESOP accounts to 401(k) accounts or other tax-qualified plan accounts, or otherwise distribute the proceeds to the participants.
2. If the buyer is an ESOP sponsor company, merge it with the buyer's ESOP.

If the ESOP is terminated, note that the participants automatically vest in all of the shares that have been allocated to their accounts. Usually, the buyer does not want to inherit the sponsor company's ESOP and the potential liabilities associated with it. Therefore, typically the buyer will choose to terminate the ESOP and transfer the participants' proceeds from the ESOP to 401(k) accounts or other tax-qualified plan accounts or otherwise distribute the proceeds to the participants, or if the buyer already has an ESOP, the buyer may choose to merge the two ESOPs.

The sale of an ESOP company can be a more complex and demanding process than the sale of a non-ESOP company. As this chapter shows, there are multiple alternatives for structuring a sale, and careful attention and qualified advice are essential to the process.

6

Legal Considerations for Buyers and Sellers of ESOP Companies

Edward C. Renenger

ESOPS, LIKE OTHER RETIREMENT PLANS, are established with an intention to be permanent. However, companies owned, in whole or in part, by an ESOP ("ESOP companies"), like non-ESOP companies, are bought and sold on a regular basis and engage in the full scope of corporate transactions. ESOP trustees have a fiduciary obligation to be open to the possibility of engaging in corporate transactions, including the sale of the company if the appropriate situation presents itself. In many ways, selling an ESOP company is no different than selling a non-ESOP company. There are, however, unique matters that arise in the course of selling an ESOP company that buyers and sellers need to consider when negotiating the transaction. The other chapters in this book explore several of these situations. This chapter discusses the legal considerations that arise in the sale of an ESOP company.

Unless otherwise noted, this chapter explores the stock sale of a middle-market ESOP company, since this represents the typical transaction involving the sale of an ESOP company.

General Background on Risk Allocation

A general understanding of risk allocation in purchases and sales of privately owned companies may be helpful before addressing the details of buying or selling an ESOP company.

In most corporate transactions, the seller is responsible for liabilities that relate to actions or conditions that occurred or arose before the sale, whereas the buyer is responsible for liabilities that relate to actions that occur or arise after the sale.[1] In practice, sellers provide statements of fact about the business and its operations, which are called "representations and warranties" (discussed in more detail below under "Representations and Warranties When Selling an ESOP Company"). The buyer, in addition to completing its own diligence, relies on these representations and warranties to understand the legal risk related to the company and its operations. In addition, the seller will provide an "indemnity" (discussed in more detail below under "Indemnification and Related Topics") to the buyer related to any breaches of these representations and warranties, which is a legal commitment by the seller to make the buyer whole for any liabilities related to such breaches.

One popular tool in sales of privately held companies is the use of insurance to help the buyer and seller insure some of the risk associated with breaches of representations and warranties and its related indemnity. This is discussed more fully below under "Representation and Warranty Insurance."

Representations and Warranties When Selling an ESOP Company

In most transactions involving the sale of a company or its assets, a potential buyer will require someone to provide representations and warranties about the company and its operations. The representations and warranties, in conjunction with the buyer's due diligence, present information about the company and its operations. Addition-

1. There are limitations to this risk allocation that are negotiated in transactions, particularly with respect to dollar amounts and time covered, which are not relevant for this introductory discussion.

ally, the representations and warranties place risk on the party who receives the proceeds of the sale by imposing liability for breaches of the representations and warranties, as explained in more detail below when discussing indemnification. Finally, true, accurate, and complete representations and warranties also serve as a condition to closing in transactions where there is an executory period between signing the transaction agreement and closing the transaction, thereby giving the buyer an opportunity to walk away from the deal or renegotiate in the event that the buyer discovers a material issue that was not properly disclosed. The representations and warranties, along with the corresponding disclosure schedules, are crucial parts of a sale transaction. They are very detailed, which is why they take up a surprisingly large portion of the relevant purchase or merger agreement.

In many closely held middle-market companies, majority shareholders are in a position to know or ascertain whether the representations and warranties are true, accurate, and complete. ESOP trustees, on the other hand, are generally not involved in the company's operations and consider the ESOP to be a stockholder that has a passive investment in the company. As such, an ESOP trustee may prefer not to make representations and warranties about the company and its operations even though there is no legal prohibition to doing so. From the buyer's perspective, this can be a challenge and lead to protracted negotiations or anxiety if the buyer does not feel confident of adequately understanding or hedging against the risk of the transaction. In some cases, the buyer may even seek to effectively hold more in reserve for unknown risk by paying less or placing more in escrow. In this sense, an ESOP-owned company is very similar to a publicly traded company, where the owners are truly passive investors and thus cannot make such representations and warranties.

Representations and warranties do not exist in a vacuum. Most transaction agreements have extensive "disclosure schedules" that permit the seller to list several items that are exceptions to, or provide additional detail about, the representations and warranties. It is common for disclosure schedules for ESOP companies to be fairly sparse. This is a mistake. ESOP trustees should require extensive disclosure schedules to mitigate against possible liability and the risk of a transaction not closing, as disclosed items are not subject to indemnification claims.

Indemnification and Related Topics

Because the buyer uses the representation and warranty provisions of the applicable agreement in part to shift risk, it will typically require the seller to indemnify the buyer for any misstatements in the representations and warranties or exceptions thereto that are not disclosed in the disclosure schedules. Indemnification is a legal concept whereby one party makes a legally binding commitment to cover any losses and expense that arise from and are related to the misstatement. In other words, the seller promises to cover any harm due to the seller's incorrect or incomplete disclosure. For example, if a liability arises that should have been disclosed in the agreement but was not, then the buyer overpaid, and it is only fair for the seller to reimburse the buyer for this liability.

Indemnity Limited to Escrow

Most ESOP trustees and their counsel take the position that the ESOP is permitted to indemnify the buyer, but prefer that indemnification claims will be capped and limited solely to amounts placed in escrow. An escrow is an amount deducted from the purchase price and held by a third-party escrow agent, who may use the escrow only for purposes of satisfying indemnity claims pursuant to a detailed escrow agreement. Most buyers insist on an escrow for the transaction so that there is a ready source of funds to satisfy any breaches of the representations and warranties, rather than relying solely on an unsecured promise to pay. If there is money left in the escrow account and there are no unresolved claims following a fixed period of time (typically 12 to 24 months following the closing of the transaction but sometimes longer), then such funds will be returned to the sellers, typically in proportion to their ownership interests at the time of the sale or as provided in the applicable agreement. By requiring indemnity claims to be limited solely to amounts in escrow, the ESOP trustee is effectively capping the potential post-closing exposure so that the ESOP's participants and beneficiaries cannot be liable for any exposure beyond such amounts. This is another example of how selling an ESOP company is similar to selling a publicly traded company, since the shareholders in a publicly traded company have no post-closing exposure.

The purported reason why ESOP trustees claim that indemnification must be limited to amounts placed in escrow is due to the prohibited transaction rules of the Internal Revenue Code of 1986, as amended (the "Code") and the Employee Retirement Income Security Act of 1974, as amended (ERISA). The prohibited transaction rules prohibit, among other things, certain direct or indirect transactions between a plan and a "disqualified person" (the term used by the Code) or a "party in interest" (the term used by ERISA).[2] Of relevance for indemnification, the Code and ERISA prohibit a direct or indirect lending of money or other extension of credit between the plan and a party in interest. The concern is that if indemnification permits a buyer to recover from the assets in the ESOP trust, then the buyer, who perhaps could be a party in interest, has extended credit to the ESOP trust or vice versa. Because of this risk, ESOP trustees generally refuse to permit the buyer to seek indemnification from the ESOP trust. There is, however, an important exception to this general limitation of indemnity risk to escrow assets as it relates to breaches of "fundamental" representations and warranties, which generally are not limited to assets held in escrow, even in sales of ESOP companies. Fundamental representations and warranties are negotiated in each transaction but generally focus on items such as the capacity of the party to enter into the transaction, authority to enter into the transaction, ownership of the shares, capital stock, and ownership of assets. The recent trend has been for buyers to try and expand the basket of "fundamental" representations to items such as environmental or ERISA compliance, particularly in purchases of ESOP companies by private equity firms.

Representation and Warranty Insurance

One tool for dealing with indemnification for ESOP companies is representation and warranty insurance, which is insurance individually underwritten to pay claims related to breaches of representations and warranties. Such insurance policies will have a fairly low retention or deductible, typically around 1% of the enterprise value of the seller at

2. Although there are minor differences between the Code's use of the term "disqualified person" and ERISA's use of the term "party in interest," such differences are not material for purposes of this chapter, so both terms are used interchangeably.

the time of writing. In an ESOP transaction, this is the amount that would typically be placed in escrow to cover payment of the retention, if needed, although in some transactions the buyer and seller will negotiate splitting the retention between the parties. Premiums for the insurance policy are currently running 3%–4% of the limit of coverage that is being purchased, and payment of such premiums is typically a matter of negotiation between buyer and seller, although the recent trend has been for such premiums to be split between the buyer and the seller. In addition, there are underwriting costs for getting the policy in place, but such costs are generally low. Finally, there are limitations of coverage and exclusions that should be carefully reviewed in any specific transaction.

In many cases, using representation and warranty insurance will result in more net consideration being paid to the ESOP at closing than solely using an escrow arrangement. Representation and warranty insurance, once fairly uncommon and reserved for very large deals, has become fairly standard for sale transactions, including sales of ESOP companies, but there are minimum sizes below which the use of such insurance is not economical. Although the size limit is a moving target, we have seen deals as small as $20 million effectively use representation and warranty insurance.

Indemnity Considerations for Asset Sales

When selling a company, the buyer and seller will negotiate as to form of the sale: a sale of stock or a sale of assets. The two primary differences between a stock sale and an asset sale are who the seller is and what is being sold. In a stock sale, the seller is the shareholder (the ESOP trustee in the case of an ESOP-owned company), and it is stock of the company that is being purchased/sold. In an asset sale, the seller is the corporation itself, and it is selling all of its assets; although the shareholders must approve the transaction, they are not directly a party to the transaction.

In a stock sale, the proceeds of the sale are paid directly to the ESOP since the ESOP trustee is the seller, whereas in an asset sale, the proceeds are instead paid to the selling corporation. In the case of an asset sale, this means that someone from the company must continue to be involved post-transaction to wind down the business, settle the claims of creditors, and ultimately dissolve. As part of this process, most of the proceeds will end up being paid to the ESOP trust as a shareholder distribution and then ultimately distributed to ESOP participants and beneficiaries, but this requires an extra step.

Regardless of whether the transaction is structured as a stock or an asset sale, the buyer is purchasing an ongoing operating company and expects to protect their risk via indemnity. In an asset sale, however, the ESOP is remaining behind and is not being acquired in the transaction, so this mitigates some of the risk of the buyer. There may also be certain liabilities excluded from the sale. The buyer, however, may still require an indemnity regime focused on protecting the downside risk for breaches of representations and warranties, including the use of an escrow.

In our experience, more ESOP company sales tend to be stock sales rather than asset sales. This is because the trustee generally has complete authority to complete a stock sale, while an asset sale will usually require an ESOP participant vote to approve the sale. The aversion to a participant vote is generally not rooted in concern that the sale will be approved but rather the time and participant disclosures required for the vote.

The size of the escrows may not be very different between stock sales and asset sales as buyers generally want both recourse and "skin in the game" from sellers regardless of the form of the sale. Buyers may also negotiate about how much of the assets from the sale remain on the corporate balance sheet instead of being distributed to the ESOP as the shareholder so that these assets remain a ready source of liquidity in the event of a breach of a representation or a warranty.

Escrow Considerations in Valuation

The use of an escrow account to settle indemnity claims raises a question: Is the purchase price the stated purchase price or the stated purchase price minus the amount placed in escrow? This question is very important for the trustee to answer, in consultation with its financial advisor, who is engaged by the trustee to complete an interim valuation of the company and issue an opinion that the terms of the transaction, taken as a whole, are fair to the ESOP from a financial point of view. That is because ERISA requires that the consideration received in the transaction must be no less than "adequate consideration" as defined in ERISA Section 3(18). In determining the transaction price, most ESOP appraisers take the position that only consideration that is not at risk for indemnity claims should be considered when determining whether the ESOP received adequate consideration. As such, the assets held in the escrow account are sometimes not considered for this analysis.

ERISA does not require a trustee or appraiser to exclude the value of the escrow account from its determination of adequate consideration. If the escrow account, or a portion thereof, will not be excluded from determining adequate consideration, then the trustee and the appraiser should be able to provide justification for why the escrow was not completely excluded from their adequate consideration analysis. For example, the appraiser could survey available industry information for indemnity claims to determine what percentage of escrow assets is typically paid to sellers to determine what ratio should apply to the analysis. There are, however, no formally approved methods of making this determination. Many appraisers and trustees, therefore, prefer to exclude the entire value of the escrow account from the analysis since this presents little risk that they overvalued the transaction consideration for fiduciary purposes.

The exclusion of the escrow account from the adequate consideration analysis can make negotiating a transaction more difficult for both buyer and seller. Most sophisticated buyers and sellers recognize that if full disclosure has been made and risks properly valued, all or a large percentage of the escrow account will likely be returned to the sellers, and the escrow acts as an "insurance policy" for claims that were not envisioned. Because the treatment of the escrow account by most appraisers and trustees is at odds with conventional transactions, the parties may have a different perspective of the total deal value.

For example, assume a $150 million transaction with $15 million of that amount set aside in an escrow account. Most buyers believe that they are paying $150 million for the company but require that the seller set aside $15 million of that amount to reimburse the buyer if there is a claim that reduces the value of the company by this amount. Most sellers look at it the same way. An ESOP seller, however, may view this transaction very differently. The ESOP seller instead may look at this as a transaction for $135 million with a potential for up to $15 million more if there are no claims. This different viewpoint complicates negotiations, especially if all or a portion of the $15 million is the difference between whether the trustee and appraiser can determine that the sales price satisfies the adequate consideration requirement. To the extent that the ESOP has engaged a qualified investment banker to run a competitive process for selling the company, as discussed in the chapter "Evaluating Offers to ESOP Companies: The Case for Engaging an Investment Banker" in this book, these issues can be negotiated more easily because the market process provides strong evidence that the adequate consideration requirement was met.

Joint and Several Indemnification

Where the ESOP is the sole recipient of the transaction proceeds, the ESOP, through the indemnity escrow, will be solely responsible for indemnity claims. If, however, the ESOP is not the sole owner of the company's stock, or there are other parties, such as warrant holders, who have a financial interest in the transaction, indemnification becomes more complicated.

The buyer's favored approach to indemnification when there is more than one shareholder is to require the sellers to provide joint and several indemnification for breaches of representations and warranties. Joint and several liability is a legal concept that provides that the harmed party (the buyer in this case) can seek total recovery from any party (any seller in this case), who is then required to individually satisfy the complete liability and seek recovery from other parties, if applicable. Joint and several liability does not work when the ESOP trust is one of several parties to a sales transaction.

If the ESOP is one of several owners and is party to an agreement that requires joint and several liability, then the ESOP could be liable for 100% of an indemnification claim even though it was not the 100% recipient of the transaction proceeds. This situation is impermissible under the prohibited transaction rules discussed above because the ESOP could be indirectly providing an extension of credit to the other shareholders since it could legally be liable for all indemnity claims.

Rather than joint and several liability, an ESOP trustee will instead require that the representations and warranties and any related indemnification are several rather than joint and several. This means that each party is separately liable for its share of the indemnification claim in proportion to the proceeds that each party received in the transaction. For example, if there were two owners, a 60% majority owner and a 40% ESOP owner, under several liability, the majority owner would be liable for only 60% of the indemnity claim and the ESOP would be liable for only 40% of the indemnity claim.

Earnouts

One tool used by buyers to help bridge potential gaps in a purchase price negotiation is to potentially pay more consideration via an earnout. An earnout is an additional payment(s) made by the buyer to the seller after the transaction closes and typically is contingent on future performance of the seller, such as hitting certain revenue or profitability targets in the current or future accounting period(s). These payments are made after the applicable performance target is hit, which is typically no later than 12 to 24 months following the close of the transaction. Earnouts for the sale of ESOP companies present challenges for ESOP trustees in the same manner as escrows because of uncertainty in valuing the earnout; some advisors view an earnout as a potential prohibited transaction because, unlike an escrow, it effectively extends credit to a potential party in interest. Earnouts are rarely used in stock sales of ESOP companies but may be used in asset sales where necessary to complete a transaction.

Sellers' Representative

When there are several shareholders in a sale, most buyers prefer to work with a single person or entity for matters that arise after closing, such as approval of indemnity claims or releases of the escrow. This person is typically referred to as a sellers' representative since they are tasked with representing the interests of all sellers. Most ESOP trustees take the position that the sellers' representative cannot represent the ESOP's interest because the ESOP must make its own decisions.

The primary reason for this is because the trustee does not believe that ERISA's fiduciary requirements permit the trustee to delegate its discretion on post-closing matters even though there are no explicit prohibitions on the use of a sellers' representative. Because of this, it is typically necessary for the buyer to get comfortable with the idea of working with two parties: the ESOP trustee, and a sellers' representative who will represent the non-ESOP sellers.

Working Capital

Broadly speaking, working capital is the difference between current assets and current liabilities. The buyer and seller agree on what level of working capital is needed for the ongoing operations of the company. This target level of operating liquidity, or working capital, is often heavily negotiated between buyer and seller. Due to the fact that the components of working capital often fluctuate on a monthly, seasonal, or other basis, it is quite common for the company's balance sheet at closing to vary from the agreed-upon level of working capital. As such, there will often be adjustments after closing to ensure that the company has the agreed-upon level of working capital. Where the balance sheet is stronger than the target level of working capital, this results in an adjustment in favor of the seller. Where the balance sheet is weaker than the target level of working capital, this results in an adjustment in favor of the buyer. For the same reasons described above regarding the use of an escrow account to satisfy indemnity claims, ESOP sellers will require that there is a working capital escrow account to satisfy potential working capital adjustments after closing. For the same reasons discussed earlier related to a sellers' representative and joint and several indemnification, the ESOP trustee will typically require that any adjustments in favor of the buyer will be on a several (rather than joint and several) basis and that the trustee retains discretion to approve adjustments rather than rely on a sellers' representative.

Closing Thoughts

Although ESOP companies are bought and sold on a regular basis, such transactions present unique legal and structuring considerations that are not present in transactions that do not involve ownership by an ESOP. For buyers who do not have an ESOP or do not have ESOP experience, this additional complexity may appear to be a barrier to a successful transaction. On the other hand, if the parties have advisors experienced with ESOP transactions and are proactive in addressing the unique issues involved in buying and selling an ESOP company, the issues are addressable and can even provide informed buyers a competitive advantage over less experienced suitors and can enable sellers to maximize net proceeds while minimizing risk.

7

Employee Relations Issues in ESOP Company Sales

Corey Rosen

THE SALE OF A COMPANY can be a great opportunity for employees to gain a substantial premium on their ESOP ownership. There are stories of ESOP participants who have cashed out well into six figures and been able to buy a new house, retire, or pursue a new career they have always wanted to try. But even with the most successful ESOPs, the primary focus of many employees will be on whether they get a job with the acquiring company and what kind of employer that company will be. If the company is not one where there are a lot of people with large account balances, then just about everyone will be in this boat, and where the company is selling because it is in trouble, employee anxiety will be running high.

Companies manage the employee relations issues in acquisitions in a variety of ways. A few are open enough to let people know that the company is looking to be acquired. Most others don't say anything, or wait until a possible sale is fairly well along, but rumors often start to fly anyway. A larger number of companies allow employees to vote on the acquisition, whether on a legally binding or an advisory basis.

However a company handles the pre-sale communications and discussions, it is essential to handle the post-sale communications openly and in detail. This is a time of great uncertainty and often anxiety for employees. They will want information and credible reassurances that the sale process was managed for their benefit. They especially will want to know when they will get their distributions and what, if any, contingencies there are on them. They will want to know whatever you can tell them about their possible employment with the new company. Taking extra measures on communications is what we would expect of employee ownership companies, but it also can help assure that the handover will go well and will lessen the possibility of future litigation.

Communicating Corporate Policy on Being Acquired

Long before a company even considers being sold, it should communicate to employees what its policy is on being acquired. There is no requirement to do this. But it can greatly enhance the credibility of the ownership plan. This kind of discussion tells employees they can be treated as adults and that any sale will be carefully vetted to protect their interests,

What and how to communicate will depend on the company's policy, but assume that the policy is the typical one for a company that takes its ESOP seriously. Ideally, the company has the kind of written policy statement described in the first chapter of this book or at least has a clear, if informal, understanding at the board level that the company is not being managed for sale, and that the intention is to stay an independent, employee-owned company. However, given the right circumstances or a compelling offer, a sale would be seriously considered.

In this case, it would make sense to discuss with employees several key issues:

- Why is the company being managed to stay employee-owned, and what does this mean in terms of strategy and culture? Is the idea to reinvest profits for growth, or is it to focus on existing markets to improve (and possibly periodically pay out) profits? How is the role of an employee as a long-term owner different than in a conventional company in terms of rights, responsibilities, information sharing, and opportunities to have input?

- What happens when an unsolicited bidder makes an offer? Explain who makes the decision, why most such offers are not serious, what requirements the board will have for a potential unsolicited bidder, and why it can be very difficult for an unwanted sale to occur (such as that there usually needs to be a very high premium and the buyer faces long and complex legal hurdles that are not an issue in a non-ESOP purchase, for instance). Explain that unwanted acquisitions in ESOP companies almost never occur—in fact, there have only been a handful over the last few decades.
- Explain what might prompt a company either to seek a buyer or respond positively to an offer. Reasons can include a premium too good to turn down, the need for more capital to grow the business, a downturn in the company's fortunes, unplanned financial liabilities, and possibly others.
- Explain what happens when a buyer is being taken seriously. Discuss how first the board must determine whether it is in the interest of the shareholders, is financially sound, and does not contain unacceptable conditions. Then talk about what happens if the offer goes to the ESOP fiduciary. Describe how the fiduciary will get an independent assessment of the fairness of the transaction, how the fiduciary will work to negotiate the best deal possible, and why the fiduciary cannot legally make a decision focused on protecting the interests of managers or non-ESOP owners.
- Explain that fiduciaries have to make decisions based on the long-term financial interests of employees as shareholders, not employees, because the ESOP is legally a retirement plan. Be clear, however, that this does not mean that any offer at a higher price is automatically accepted and that, instead, the fiduciary needs to compare how employees would fare over time staying at an ESOP company and what they would get from the offeror. As noted elsewhere in this book, that almost always means a very large premium.
- Finally, explain what voice, if any, employees have in the sale. Employees will wonder, of course, why the decision is not simply theirs (unless, of course, you pass through the decision to employees, albeit even then there are some constraints). Explain that the sale of an ESOP company is a complex issue, with layers of

legal obligations, detailed financial investigations, and stringent requirements on what is and is not acceptable. Having a fiduciary (preferably you can tell them it will be an independent one on this issue) who can actively negotiate the best deal is likely to generate the best outcome.

- Doing all this is likely to enhance employees' feelings of security about the ESOP and their sense that the company treats them like owners. After all, wouldn't non-ESOP owners, especially if they owned much or all of a company, want to know all this?

Communicating About a Possible Sale

Most ESOP companies will not tell employees who do not otherwise need to know that a sale is being considered. Disclosing a possible sale could lead to some people looking for other jobs, a loss of productivity as employees become anxious about their futures, rumors about what kind of sale price they will get, violations of confidentiality agreements in the negotiations process, and distractions from everyday work.

While these are compelling arguments, employees may also come to believe that a sale is in the works on their own. Visitors, often in suits, may be walking around the company asking questions. An employee who has been privy to initial discussions may be indiscreet. There may be a push to improve the appearance of the facility for no obvious reason. The CEO may seem preoccupied. If the company has been facing financial problems, people may believe a sale is the only way to be rescued. If it is clear that employees do believe a sale is being considered, stonewalling is not a good strategy. If the company has laid the groundwork on company policy about acquisitions, employees will have a reasonable context within which to evaluate what is going on. There will still be stress and anxiety, but less than if all they know is rumors. This is especially true since research shows that in most groups, negative people are seen as smarter (and are usually more vocal) than positive ones, so the rumors are likely to be worse than the reality.

In some companies, however, there may be a more proactive strategy to seek employee input beforehand. There might be an advisory vote, focus groups, an all-employee meeting, or other mechanism to keep people informed at the outset of any serious offer, with periodic updates on what is happening. We at the NCEO would recommend this strategy only for companies with very strong ownership cultures and trust levels, and then only for very serious offers. Check with legal counsel, however, about what information can and cannot be disclosed.

Employee Voting

As noted elsewhere, if the company's bylaws require it, or the sale is structured as a merger or asset sale, an employee vote is normally required, although the fiduciary could override it if the vote clearly conflicts with ERISA. We have yet to witness a case like this in a closely held company, however.

There are specific legal requirements for disclosure before a vote. Essentially, employees must be given enough financial information well enough in advance (30 days or more typically) to make an informed choice. The information should be understandable, although that is a difficult thing to do with material like this, and courts would not expect miracles. Above all, it should be impartial, meaning it is essential to have it prepared by an outside firm expert in this area. The material should also be very clear about how and when to vote.

Issues When the Sale is Completed

We get a lot of calls at the NCEO from employees in ESOP companies that have been sold wondering where their money is or why it is taking so long to get it. As Nancy Dittmer explains in her chapter in this book, there are a variety of ways the assets in the ESOP can be treated in a sale. They could go into a successor retirement plan for the buyer (even their ESOP if they have one), could be paid out only after contingencies are resolved, could be paid out for shares in the acquirer if it is a public company, or could be paid out all at once or over time.

Employees need to have all this spelled out very clearly. Just giving them a document is not likely enough. Many people will not read it; those who do may not understand it. A meeting or series of meetings (ideally in smaller groups) is a far better approach. Be sure to explain why the process is what it is and the difficulties an immediate payout would raise (if this is not what will happen).

Because the amounts may be substantial for many people, it is essential (and legally required) to provide them information on the tax consequences they will face and their various options. The company should not provide financial advice, but bringing on a financial planner could be enormously helpful.

Finally, there will be a lot of employee anxiety about the new employer. If the news is good (all the jobs will be kept, for instance), the new employer would be well advised to meet with the employees and explain their futures. If this is not the case, then the ESOP company should do this. It is not a legal issue, but just to leave the matter hanging seems like cruel and unusual punishment.

8

What Can You Do If You Don't Want to Be Sold?

Corey Rosen

ESOP COMPANIES GET OFFERS all the time. This book has detailed how to respond to these offers, but what if the company wants to stay employee-owned? Can it, even in the face of an attractive offer? While there is no way to bulletproof your company from an acquisition, there are prudent and reasonable steps you can take to give you more control.

First, the board should adopt a policy on how it will respond to offers, outlining what it requires for an offer to be considered legitimate and what the process under ERISA will require of buyers. The appendices to this book contain useful sample documents for this. Buyers need to know that buying an ESOP company is a long and expensive proposition with an uncertain outcome. Many will decide not to pursue the company at this point.

Second, the board should be clear that under ERISA, the board and/or the trustee have an obligation to consider seeking additional offers. The chapter in this book on using an M&A firm in this process outlines some of the steps that might be taken. That may discourage other buyers.

Third, the board may want to ask prospective buyers to pay for due diligence. Why should a target company that may not be sold in the end pay for the considerable costs and staff time involved in due diligence when it is not seeking a buyer? Arguably, this is not just an allowable step to take but a sound one from the standpoint of not wasting corporate assets.

Fourth, be clear that you are appointing an outside trustee to act for the plan. This is clearly a best practice, but also raises the bar for the offer.

Fifth, as the chapter in this book on responding to unsolicited offers points out, the offer needs to be at a very substantial premium to be worth considering, assuming the company does not want or need to be sold because of financial or competitive constraints, such as not being able to meet its repurchase obligation.

Finally, there is the much more complicated issue of having employees vote on the transaction. If an ESOP company receives an offer to purchase substantially all its assets or stock and the directors are in favor of accepting the offer, then the ESOP trustee is required under ERISA to exercise its fiduciary duty in deciding whether to vote the ESOP shares in favor of or against the proposed transaction. In certain circumstances, ESOP participants have a right to vote on the transaction. Can they vote "no" and force the trustee to vote "no" as well?

The answer depends on the circumstances. First, if there are unallocated shares, the trustee will vote those shares unless the plan document requires mirror voting of unallocated shares based on participants' votes of allocated shares. The trustee does not necessarily have to follow these directions, however, if the trustee believes it would be a breach of fiduciary duty under ERISA to follow the participants' vote. That could happen, for instance, if the participants voted "no" on an offer with a very large premium from a buyer that would lay off employees, relocate operations, or offer continued employment but for lower compensation. Employees could be put in the difficult situation of losing their jobs or working for less pay, in return for a relatively small amount of money for their stock.

In *Herman v. NationsBank of Georgia, N.A.*, a case concerning a hostile takeover bid for Polaroid, the Department of Labor took the position that the ESOP trustee must essentially ignore participant directions if it concludes that the offer would substantially increase the value of plan assets. In a 1995 letter to the AFL-CIO, Olena Berg, the Assistant Secretary of Labor at the time, said that trustees cannot "automatically assume that following plan provisions [providing for participant voting] in every case will come out with a result that is prudent under ERISA." But in those cases where a trustee does not follow the participants' vote, the trustee needs to show in writing why it followed its own course.

Trustees ordinarily should give deference to the participants' vote but can still override it if the trustee believes the participants' decision is inconsistent with ERISA requirements. This effectively expands the range of acceptable offers. Some offers that the trustee normally might accept could be rejected, but higher offers could not be rejected if doing so would be a breach of fiduciary duty

If a company does provide for voting on the sale, participants must be given adequate disclosure materials to make their choice. The trustee (not the company) should hire an advisory firm to prepare detailed material on the offer, explaining the risks and considerations in language ordinary participants can understand. Company management needs to be exceptionally cautious to play a neutral role in this process. Management should, however, make sure that employees understand how ERISA works in acquisitions, ideally by bringing in an independent third party. Acquirers need to be told in advance, in detail, what this process will involve and how much it might cost in dollars and time.

Requiring a pass-through vote by ESOP participants may, in itself, discourage potential buyers who are not comfortable with the prospect of going through a long, expensive process of making an offer in the face of an uncertain election. Even the possibility of a "no" vote could be perceived by a potential buyer as making the acquisition of an ESOP company more expensive than a company without an ESOP.

APPENDIX

A

Sample Company Acquisition Policy

James G. Steiker

Disclaimer: *This document is merely a sample form. Readers should consult with counsel to adopt an appropriate policy and related communications on behalf of a company.*

Dear __________:

Thank you for your inquiry concerning your interest in acquiring all of the stock or assets of ______. Our board of directors has determined generally that a sale of the company is not in the best interests of shareholders at this time.

We acknowledge, however, a duty to consider serious and bona fide offers. Our board has adopted a policy with respect to unsolicited inquiries such as yours. We do not respond generally to unsolicited inquiries or share company financial or other information other than to inform the inquirer of our policy. Our policy further requires that we will consider whether to engage in further discussions and provide additional information only upon receipt of the following detailed information:

1. The identity of the proposed acquirer and all related parties;
2. Proposed preliminary acquisition terms, including price, key representations and warranties, and terms of payment of the purchase price;

3. Detailed information concerning the financial capability of the acquirer to complete the transaction;
4. The effect of the proposed acquisition on current company operations, management, and employees;
5. The industry experience of the acquirer;
6. Examples of prior successful acquisitions by the acquirer; and
7. The key elements of the acquirer's business plan upon acquisition of the company.

   [For 100% ESOP-owned S corporations]
8. State how the proposed acquisition will provide more value to company shareholders over the next 5 years than continued operation of the company as a 100% ESOP-owned S corporation.

   [For benefit corporations]
9. State how the prospective acquiring company's proposed acquisition terms, values, and beliefs fit with the company's election as a benefit corporation and related benefit purposes.

Upon receipt of the information and offer meeting the conditions above, the board may then consider whether to (i) commence formal discussions regarding the offer, and/or (ii) engage an outside financial advisor to provide advice with respect to the offer and to conduct a sale process to solicit other offers. We provide no assurance, however, that the company will engage in any further discussion with you or provide any further information after receipt of such information and offer. That determination will be made based upon the board's evaluation as to whether such discussion is in the best interests of shareholders. Generally, any proposed sale of the company will be subject to both board and shareholder approval, and we can provide no assurance that the shareholders of the company will approve a proposed sale even if such sale is approved by the board.

We appreciate your consideration of our policies in this matter.

Sincerely,

____

APPENDIX
B

Sample Questions to Ask Potential Acquirers

This document was contributed to the NCEO by an anonymous ESOP company that was in the process of being acquired.

In addition to providing us with relevant financials for your company (income statement, balance sheet, and details on how this transaction will be financed), please let us know:

- Why would COMPANY NAME be a fit for you?
- What is your approach to setting compensation and benefit levels? For instance, do you aim at offering comparable wages and benefits as competitors do, or do you have a different approach?
- Please describe your current retirement and health plans for your employees.
- What is your target compensation for corporate officers? How much is in incentive pay?
- How would you describe your culture? What role, if any, do nonmanagement employees have in providing input or making decisions about their own jobs?
- What will happen to the COMPANY NAME brand?
- Is there a formal onboarding approach our team members would work through as we transition from COMPANY NAME to the new entity? Can you briefly describe it?
- What opportunities exist for growing COMPANY NAME as a part of your company?

- Do you pay bonuses or other incentives? What are they based on?
- What are opportunities to use corporate resources such as accounting, HR, IT, administration, sales, and service? Would using these replace such services provided by us?
- What are the expectations from investors or owners for their own liquidity over the next several years?
- Does your strategic plan envision looking to find an attractive buyer at some point in the near to mid-term?
- What are growth goals for the stock value?
- Does your company make stock available to employees? Which ones and in what way?
- Do you expect to do other acquisitions in the next 5 to 10 years?
- What is the corporate EBITDA goal?

APPENDIX

C

Key ESOP Issues: Informational Letter to a Potential Acquirer

This document, which details the legal steps a company must take when considering an offer, can be used as an informational letter sent to a potential acquirer. The goal is to make sure the would-be acquirer understands the potential costs and complexity of the proposed transaction.

XXX is a YYY% employee stock ownership plan (ESOP)-owned company. ESOPs are organized under the Employee Retirement Income Security Act (ERISA) and Internal Revenue Code. As such, they are governed by very specific statutory and case law regarding how we can respond to an acquisition offer.

The shares in the ESOP are held in trust. The trust is considered the single owner of the shares. The trustee votes and, if appropriate, tenders the shares held by the plan. The trustee is appointed by the board of directors. The trustee is required by law to act for the "exclusive benefit of plan participants." Case law has clarified that in the case of an acquisition offer, the trustee must determine that participants would be better off over a period of time, usually three to seven years, selling their shares to an acquirer and reinvesting the proceeds at market rates than they would be if the company were not sold. Projected future values for ESOP accounts include both appreciation on the shares and expected contributions to the ESOP in excess of normal retirement contributions by companies. If the offer exceeds this expected value, the trustee will consider it.

There are several steps in the process of responding to an offer:

- If the CEO believes that an offer is serious and merits consideration by the board, the board will evaluate the offer. The board will normally hire its own investment advisor. The board may decide to reject the offer if it believes it would not be likely to meet the criteria for the trustee laid out above. If that is not the case, the board may decide to solicit other bids as well.
- For bids the board believes the trustee must consider under the requirements of ERISA, the board will follow normal best practices to assess the offer, including assessing the financing, structure, and terms of the offer; meeting with officers of the potential acquirer; and assessing how the acquisition would affect the employees and corporate culture.
- For offers that continue to meet the basic ERISA criteria, the board will then turn the decision over to the trustee.
- If the current trustee is not an independent outside trustee (as opposed to one or more insiders), the board will appoint an independent transactional trustee.
- The trustee will do its own analysis and may ask the board to solicit additional information and/or offers.
- The trustee will hire its own legal and financial advisors, including a financial advisor to perform a fairness opinion. The fairness opinion is an assessment of the fairness of the transaction to ESOP participants relative to any other parties to the sale.
- The trustee will then conduct negotiations with the potential buyer(s) over the terms and structure of the transaction, leading to a final decision on whether to proceed.
- If the transaction is structured as an asset sale, employees must be able to direct the trustee as to the disposition of the assets. Proxy material compliant with ERISA and securities laws will need to be developed for this process. Otherwise, the trustee makes the final determination. *[Companies with full pass-through voting rights should amend this section to say that employees will be asked to vote on any sale offer.]*

In a typical case, the process will last several months.

About the Authors

Neil Brozen is the president of Ventura ESOP Fiduciary Services, a nationwide provider of independent ESOP trustee services. He began providing ESOP trustee services in 2005 for BNC Bank and was instrumental in helping Bankers Trust Company become a national player from 2010 to April 2016. He began providing individual trustee services in the summer of 2016. He has been responsible for managing more than 300 ESOP transactions and almost 200 ongoing ESOPs. Neil serves on the Employee Ownership Expansion Network's board, the Employee-Owned S Corporations of America's Advisory Committee, and the ESOP Association's Advisory Committee on Fiduciary Issues. He previously served on the NCEO's board of directors and the ESOP Association's board of governors. He is a frequent national speaker on various ESOP issues and has contributed to several NCEO publications. Neil is extremely passionate about employee ownership. He previously worked for the IRS, Arthur Andersen & Co., and several private companies, and had his own management consulting firm.

Tabitha Croscut is a shareholder and director at Devine, Millimet & Branch, P.A., with a national legal practice focused on ESOPs as ownership succession and employee compensation strategies for privately held companies. Tabitha counsels her clients regarding transactional, compliance, and fiduciary issues with respect to their ESOPs, and represents companies, sellers, and internal and external trustees. Tabitha serves as a director of the Vermont Employee Ownership Center (VEOC); is a member of the National Center for Employee Ownership (NCEO) and the ESOP Association (TEA), serving on TEA's Legislative & Regulatory Committee; and serves on the board of trustees for the Employee Ownership Foundation.

Nancy Dittmer is a senior vice president at Newport Group, a retirement services firm, and is located in the West Des Moines, Iowa, office. Nancy has over 30 years of experience in the employee benefits field and provides feasibility studies, repurchase obligation forecasting, annual participant accounting and reporting, and Internal Revenue Code Section 409(p) testing for clients. Nancy, who earned her bachelor's degree in business administration from Iowa State University, has been a frequent author and speaker at national ESOP conferences. Her professional affiliations include the ESOP Association (TEA) and serving as the past chair of TEA's Advisory Committee on Administration; the National Center for Employee Ownership (NCEO) and writing for NCEO's publications and website; the American Institute of Certified Public Accountants and the Iowa Society of CPAs; and serving on Iowa State University College of Business Dean's Advisory Council and as an Iowa State University Foundation governor.

Alex Perry, ASA, is a director with Ventura ESOP Fiduciary Services. Before joining Ventura in 2018, he spent eight years providing valuation and financial advisory services for closely held businesses, primarily in connection with ESOPs as well as for financial reporting, gift and estate, and incentive plan purposes. Alex is an Accredited Senior Appraiser in business valuation and is a member of the NCEO, the ESOP Association, and the American Society of Appraisers.

Ed Renenger, president and CEO of SES ESOP Strategies and co-chair of the Stevens & Lee ESOP and employee benefits and compensation groups, focuses on helping companies navigate ESOP complexities. Ed advises owners on selling their companies to employees through an ESOP and on ESOP-related transactions. He works with S corporations, C corporations, public and private companies, ESOP trust-owned companies, and minority ESOP companies. Ed also counsels ESOP trustees on ERISA obligations and issues with established ESOPs.

Corey Rosen is the NCEO's founder and former executive director and now is its senior staff member. Corey has spoken on various subjects related to employee ownership all over the world with government, business, and union leaders, and he is regularly quoted in leading magazines and newspapers. He has appeared on national television and radio programs and also has authored four books on employee ownership, plus more than 100 articles for various business, academic, and professional publications. He has authored or coauthored several of the NCEO's practical and research publications. He holds a PhD in political science from Cornell University.

Mark Russell, the head of the finance group for SES ESOP Strategies and a senior managing director at Griffin Financial Group, helps ESOP-owned companies conduct a competitive sale process. Mark also helps companies determine the feasibility of an ESOP and whether an ESOP is the appropriate vehicle for the relevant stakeholders. Where the ESOP is not the right fit, Mark assists owners in determining what alternative structure is more appropriate.

Randolph R. Smith, Jr., is an ESOP attorney and a partner with SmithLynch, LLC, in Atlanta, GA. He represents ESOP companies, selling shareholders, ESOP trustees, and lenders in multi-million dollar leveraged ESOP buyouts, and related corporate restructurings and financings. He also specializes in representing ESOP companies, ESOP trustees, buyers, and other parties in the sale of ESOP companies.

James G. Steiker is the chair of SES ESOP Strategies, a Stevens & Lee/Griffin Platform company. He is a corporate, pension, and tax attorney and financial advisor with more than 35 years of experience in ESOPs and other employee ownership matters. He focuses his practice primarily on ESOP design, transactions, and compliance in entrepreneurial companies. Jim has served on the ESOP Association's board of governors and is a past chair of the ESOP Association's Advisory Committee on Finance. He is also a trustee of the Employee Ownership Foundation and a former member of the board of directors of the National Center for Employee Ownership. He is a director of the Employee Ownership Expansion Network and also serves as a director of seven ESOP companies.

About the NCEO

The National Center for Employee Ownership (NCEO) is a nonprofit organization that has supported the employee ownership community since 1981. Our mission is to help employee ownership thrive. We have more than 3,000 members because we help people make smart decisions about employee ownership, with everything from reliable information on technical issues to helping companies reach the full potential of employee ownership. We continuously work to:

- produce practical resources for employee-owned companies;
- conduct research on ESOPs, including showing the economic benefits of employee ownership;
- facilitate the exchange of best practices at our live and online events;
- feature the best and most current writing by experts in our publications;
- advise lawmakers on the best ways to encourage employee ownership;
- help employee ownership companies build ownership cultures where employees think and act like owners;
- and do much more—join today if you are not already a member.

Membership Benefits

NCEO members receive the following benefits and more:

- The members-only newsletter *Employee Ownership Report*.
- Access to the NCEO's members-only website resources, including the ESOP Q&A, the ESOP Lender Directory, and more.

- Access to downloads of sample documents and checklists on essential ESOP topics.
- Free access to both live and recorded webinars.
- Networking opportunities at educational events.
- Discounts on books and other NCEO products and services.
- The right to contact the NCEO for answers to questions.

How to Join or Order This Book

To join or order publications, visit us online at www.nceo.org, where you also can find a wide variety of resources on employee ownership.

To order this book, go to www.nceo.org/r/offers (if you are not already a member but join in the same order, you will receive the member discount on the book).

Made in United States
North Haven, CT
03 November 2026

21721425R00065